THE
DON'T SWEAT
THE SMALL STUFF
WORKBOOK

Don't Sweat the Small Stuff with Your Family

Don't Worry, Make Money

Don't Sweat the Small Stuff . . . and It's All Small Stuff

Slowing Down to the Speed of Life
(with Joseph Bailey)

Handbook for the Heart
(with Benjamin Shield)

Handbook for the Soul
(with Benjamin Shield)

Shortcut Through Therapy

You Can Feel Good Again

You Can Be Happy No Matter What

THE
DON'T SWEAT
THE SMALL STUFF
WORKBOOK

SIMPLE WAYS TO KEEP THE LITTLE THINGS

FROM TAKING OVER YOUR LIFE

Richard Carlson, Ph.D.

HYPERION

New York

ISBN: 0-7868-8351-0

Designed by Jennifer Ann Daddio

FIRST EDITION

3   5   7   9   10   8   6   4

Contents

Introduction

I am extremely grateful for the warm reception to my book *Don't Sweat the Small Stuff*. Millions of people have taken the message to heart and are attempting to put the ideas into practice to become kinder, wiser, happier, more patient, and less stressed individuals. I have been blessed by thousands of kind letters from readers expressing their thanks and sharing their stories. Many readers have shared with me the various ways that they have learned to stop sweating the small stuff in their own lives. Some are funny; many are incredibly moving. It seems that almost everyone has their own favorite strategies from the book that have had a particularly positive impact on their life.

In addition to all the letters, I have met countless people all across the country during book signings and lectures. Time and time again, I have been asked if it would be possible to create a workbook to make it a little easier to put the concepts into practice. Because many people *do* learn best through exercises, and because I have always tried very hard to listen to what my readers are saying, it is my privilege to introduce you to *The Don't Sweat the Small Stuff Workbook*.

Each of you will undoubtedly feel that certain strategies from *Don't Sweat the Small Stuff* seem more difficult than others to put into practice. While you may intuitively know that particular strategies would be beneficial to your life, you may need a little help in reinforcing them. My suggestion is this: Take a few moments to reread and reflect upon the entire strategy you are contemplating. When you are finished, open this workbook to the parallel strategy and begin the exercise.

I hope you will approach this workbook in the same lighthearted spirit in which it has been written. In other words, while you certainly want to practice the suggestions and do the best you can to incorporate the material into your daily life, I encourage you to do so with a smile on your face. Avoid "keeping score" of how you are doing or making too big a deal out of any individual exercise. You certainly don't want to "sweat" *The Don't Sweat the Small Stuff Workbook*! As is true with the original book, the strategies are designed to help you put things into perspective and make the most of the tremendous gift of your life.

I wish you the very best of luck in taking the material from *Don't Sweat the Small Stuff* and putting it into practice in your daily life. I hope this workbook makes it easier to do so. I send you my love and very best wishes.

Treasure yourself,
Richard Carlson

1.

Don't Sweat the Small Stuff

Often we allow ourselves to get all worked up about things that, upon closer examination, *aren't* really that big a deal. We focus on little problems and concerns and blow them way out of proportion. Whether we have to listen to unfair criticism or do the lion's share of the work, it pays big dividends if we learn not to worry about little things.

Do you "sweat the small stuff"? Complete this inventory to find out. Statements are presented in sets of three. Each one has a point value. Read all three statements and decide which one best describes your situation. Then write the point value in the space beside that statement.

1. When someone has more than ten items in the express line at the grocery store, I
___ point out the person's error and suggest that he or she choose another line. (1)
___ don't let it bother me. (3)
___ get annoyed and feel sorry for someone who is so inconsiderate of others. (2)

2. The cable goes out in the middle of a long-awaited show, so I
___ shrug my shoulders and say it will be on again. (3)
___ rant and rave about how disappointed I am. (1)
___ call the cable company to report the problem. (2)

3. After purchasing food at the drive-through window, I realize my order is wrong. I
___ go back and yell at the manager and demand a refund. (1)
___ complain to everyone around me and pick at my food. (2)
___ eat my lunch and enjoy it anyway. (3)

4. Someone is talking in the movie theater. I
___ shush very loudly. (2)
___ move to a new seat. (3)
___ inform the manager. (1)

5. When I lose change in a vending machine, I
____ never kick and shake the machine, but try another one. (3)
____ sometimes kick and shake the machine, depending on how hungry I am. (2)
____ usually kick and shake the machine—I hate feeling ripped off. (1)

6. In a crowded lot, I notice that someone has parked in two spaces. I
____ leave a note on the person's car, pointing out how inconsiderate he or she is. (1)
____ entertain thoughts of scratching the car, but drive on. (2)
____ drive on until I find another parking spot. (3)

7. One morning, the paper is late. I
____ go on with my morning and decide to read the paper during dinner. (3)
____ call the distribution office to let them know. (2)
____ get frustrated and upset because my morning routine has been interrupted. (1)

8. At a restaurant, I notice that people seated after me receive their meals first. I
____ feel I am being overlooked and complain to the waitress. (2)
____ reason that my food must take longer to cook and wait patiently. (3)
____ lose my appetite and leave the restaurant. (1)

9. A person is making an illegal left-hand turn in front of me. I
____ honk my horn and make obscene gestures as I wait. (2)
____ swerve erratically into the next lane to make my point. (1)
____ deduce that the person must have a good reason to make the turn and wait patiently. (3)

10. Only one window is open at the bank, and a large line is forming. I
____ check my items to make sure my transaction won't take very long. (3)
____ roll my eyes, let out a sigh, and check my watch. (2)
____ complain loudly to the customers around me. (1)

Score: 21–30, you rarely sweat the small stuff; 11–20, you still need some practice in trying to see everything as small stuff; 1–10, you let the small stuff get to you too often. Try to relax!

2.

Make Peace with Imperfection

Whenever we want to have something a certain way, better than it already is, we are engaged in a losing battle. Rather than being grateful for what we have, we are focused on what's wrong with something and our need to fix it. Eliminate your need for perfection in all areas of your life, and you'll begin to discover the perfection in life itself.

Are you hung up on life's imperfections? Take this questionnaire to find out. You may want to recall your answers the next time you get the urge to "improve" things. For each answer, score 0 for **never**, 5 for **sometimes**, and 10 for **most of the time**.

1. When you're a guest in someone's house, do you straighten the pictures? ____
2. After a maid has cleaned your home or hotel room, do you look for dust? ____
3. After you get your car professionally washed, do you go over it yourself? ____
4. Do you look for typos or grammatical errors in reading material? ____
5. Do you mentally "correct" the outfit or makeup of people you meet? ____
6. Before you start eating in a restaurant, do you wipe the silverware? ____
7. Do you complain to a restaurant manager about the service? ____
8. Do you correct aloud other speakers' grammar or pronunciation? ____
9. Do you worry about making such mistakes in your speaking and what people will think of you if you do? ____
10. Do you analyze aloud "what's missing" from a recipe at a friend's house? ____
11. Do you worry excessively about pleasing others with your own cooking? ____
12. Do you point out to your boss minor errors in a finished project or presentation, even though they make no difference? ____
13. When you're watching a TV show or a movie, do you tell the other viewers how you would have made it differently? ____
14. Do you criticize the behavior of celebrities? ____
15. Do you mentally redecorate rooms, other than in your own house? ____

16. Are you constantly dissatisfied with the way your own living space looks? ____

17. Are you constantly dissatisfied with the way *you* look? ____

18. After you pass a tastelessly dressed person, do you comment to the person you're with? ____

19. After you attend a party, do you criticize other guests? ____

20. Do you redo unimportant things that other people have done? ____

21. Do you give unsolicited advice to people about what they should do? ____

22. When you're telling someone about a wonderful vacation, do you feel you must include the little things that went wrong? ____

23. Before you buy something, do you spend a long time trying to find the best? ____

24. After you buy something, do you worry that you didn't get the best? ____

25. Do you often straighten things (items on a desk, tools, utensils, etc.)? ____

26. Before you leave the house, do you mentally criticize your appearance? ____

27. Do you often ask friends to reassure you that something you have done is okay? ____

28. Before you fall asleep, do you think of all the things you didn't do that day? ____

29. Do you take mental inventory of your faults? ____

30. Do you find it hard to accept a compliment? ____

Score: Less than 100, you find the world a satisfying place; 100–150, you're fairly easygoing; 150–200, you may find people avoiding you; 200–250, you could be a paid critic; more than 250, yikes!

3.

Let Go of the Idea That Gentle, Relaxed People Can't Be Superachievers

One of the major reasons so many of us remain hurried, frightened, and competitive is our fear that if we were to become more peaceful and loving, we would suddenly stop achieving our goals. You can put this fear to rest by realizing that the opposite is true. When you are fearful or frantic, you immobilize yourself from your potential, not to mention enjoyment. On the other hand, when you have what you want (inner peace), you are *less* distracted by your wants, needs, desires, and concerns. These questions will give you insights into your attitudes toward achievement.

1. Do you often lose sleep worrying about work?
2. When you're with friends, do you find yourself talking about work?
3. Before you've finished one project, are you already thinking about the next one?
4. Do you put your personal life "on hold" in order to tend to business?
5. Are you jealous of other people's achievements?
6. When you've achieved a goal or obtained something you've worked hard for, do you take the time to enjoy the accomplishment?
7. Are you too busy to cultivate a hobby?
8. Do you often work through lunch?
9. Does success mean being the first to embrace the latest trend, owning the latest-model car or gadget, or having more than your neighbors?
10. Do you fear that everything you've worked for will be lost if you don't give it your constant attention?

If you've answered yes to more than half of these questions, chances are that you haven't spent time thinking about what would make you truly happy. Your hard work is distracting you from realizing what you need to find inner peace. Try this exercise to help you.

1. Make a list of the activities you've done that have given you a sense of peace or enjoyment. These can be simple things like washing your car, smelling your grandmother's roses, or visiting a country store. Don't be afraid to reach back to simpler times when you had less on your mind. List the activities here.

2. Make time to do one or two of the activities on this list. Write them into your schedule and make an appointment with yourself if you have to. The idea is to temper your work achievements with your personal life. That's what "superachievement" is all about.

3. List the qualities of superachievers.

4. List the qualities of relaxed, peaceful, and loving people.

5. In lists 3 and 4, circle the qualities that appeal to you. Strive to achieve them in your daily life.

4.

Be Aware of the Snowball Effect
of Your Thinking

Have you ever noticed how uptight you feel when you're caught up in your thinking? One thought leads to another, and yet another, until at some point, you become incredibly agitated. The solution is to notice what's happening in your head before your thoughts have a chance to build any momentum. The sooner you catch yourself in the act of building your mental snowball, the easier it is to stop.

Are you aware of the snowball effect of your thinking? If not, try the following exercise.

- Think of everything you have to do tomorrow.
- List each thought that comes to mind.
- Pay attention to the way you feel as your thoughts keep building.
- Jot down the responses (feelings, body symptoms) you have to each thought.

Thought:

Feelings/Body Symptoms:

Thought:

Feelings/Body Symptoms:

Thought:

Feelings/Body Symptoms:

Thought:

Feelings/Body Symptoms:

Thought:

Feelings/Body Symptoms:

Thought:

Feelings/Body Symptoms:

Thought:

Feelings/Body Symptoms:

Thought:

Feelings/Body Symptoms:

1. Describe how it feels to build your mental snowball. Does it give you a sense of peace and calm? Or does it make you feel even more stressed than you were when you started?

2. Look over your responses. Circle any of the feelings or body symptoms that you'd like to avoid or eliminate. For each one, write a few lines about the changes you'd like to make.

3. List some ways in which you might stop this train of thought before it has a chance to get going. For example, rather than focus on how overwhelmed you are, think of how grateful you are for remembering what needs to be done!

5.

Develop Your Compassion

Compassion involves the willingness to put yourself in someone else's shoes. It's the recognition that other people's problems, their pain and frustration, are every bit as real as our own. In recognizing this fact and trying to offer some assistance, we open our own hearts and enhance our sense of gratitude. As Mother Teresa reminds us, "We cannot do great things on this earth. We can only do small things with great love." Here are some ways to add compassion to your life.

1. Make a list of ways a person can show compassion. Some examples are sharing a smile with a stranger, helping a harried friend shop for groceries, and volunteering time at a nursing home. List at least ten more examples below.

2. What compassionate gestures have you witnessed in others? List them below.

3. Why did these gestures stay with you? What qualities about them made them special?

4. In what ways in your daily life are you not compassionate? For example, are you an aggressive driver? Do you bark when a sales clerk or server at a restaurant provides you with less-than-adequate service? Think of these situations as opportunities to practice compassion.

5. From the lists you've just made, select the compassionate gestures you've made or make regularly. Copy them here.

6. What do these gestures have in common?

7. From lists 1 and 2 above, select the gestures you've been meaning to make or would like to make, but haven't gotten around to making yet. Copy them here.

8. What do these compassionate gestures have in common? What's stopping you from making them?

9. If you find yourself resisting an attempt to perform a new compassionate gesture, take time to work up to it. Try simpler ones. Be aware of how good they make you feel and how they make others feel. Write down one or two examples of simple acts of compassion here:

10. Take time every day (and right now!) to visualize incorporating compassion into your daily life. Complete this sentence:

My next compassionate gesture will be _____.

6.

Remind Yourself That When You Die, Your "In Basket" Won't Be Empty

Often we convince ourselves that our obsession with our "to do" list is only temporary—that once we get through the list, we'll be calm, relaxed, and happy. But in reality, this rarely happens. Regardless of who you are or what you do, remember that *nothing* is more important than your own sense of inner peace and that of your loved ones. If you're obsessed with getting everything done, you'll never have a sense of well-being. Try these exercises.

1. Work expands to fill up all available time. The trick to achieving a sense of harmony is to allocate your time in a manner that's comfortable for you. Here are three "in baskets." Fill them with what you'd like to accomplish today.

| | PROFESSIONAL | |
| PRIVATE IN BASKET | IN BASKET | SOCIAL IN BASKET |

2. Realize that you're not going to be able to empty these baskets in one day. And tomorrow will bring new work to each of the baskets. That's okay. Circle items in each in basket that you want to clear out today.

3. Allocate blocks of time to each of the three in baskets. For example, you may want to work on your Professional In Basket from 9 A.M. to 5 P.M. Then from 5 P.M. to 8 P.M. may be time for you to work on your Social In Basket. Use this time to dine with friends or simply make personal calls. After that, block out some time for your Personal In Basket: Read a book, take a hot bath, or work on household chores.

4. Tomorrow, revise your three in baskets, adding new items, removing the tasks you've completed, and reprioritizing. Revise the time allocated for each task to adjust to the changing workload but try not to change them too drastically. It's best to keep a fairly consistent schedule. Over time you'll refine the blocks of time to best suit the kinds of tasks you want to accomplish. Above all, don't beat yourself up if you don't reach your daily goal. Tomorrow's a new day. Write down one goal you wish to accomplish:

5. If you start to feel overwhelmed by all that you have to do, take a deep breath and answer these questions:

    a. Which of these tasks is most urgent?

    b. Which tasks can I accomplish fastest?

    c. If I can't get this work done, what will the consequences be?

    d. If I had been on vacation when this emergency occurred, wouldn't someone else have handled it? Would it have waited until I returned?

Once you've worked through these questions, you'll find that you can move much of what's in your in basket to your out basket with very little effort—and that many of the urgent tasks aren't so urgent after all.

Tip for keeping on top of things: Date each item in your in basket. Jobs that weren't urgent a month ago may become emergencies if they sit in your in basket for too long.

7.

Don't Interrupt Others or Finish Their Sentences

Think about it. When you hurry someone along, interrupt someone, or finish his or her sentence, you have to keep track not only of your own thoughts but of those of the person you are interrupting. It's exhausting! It's also the cause of many arguments, because if there's one thing almost everyone resents, it's someone who doesn't listen to what they are saying.

Do you interrupt others or finish their sentences? Assess yourself in social and professional situations. Read the statements below. Circle T (**true**) or F (**false**) according to whether or not each statement applies to you. Be sure to respond as you are right now, not as you'd like to be.

I often feel annoyed at someone whose pattern of speech is slower than mine.	**T**	**F**
I'm usually much too busy at work to stop and take time for a friendly chat.	**T**	**F**
I wish people would just get straight to the point and not go on and on.	**T**	**F**
I have no patience for idle conversation during the workday—or at any other time.	**T**	**F**
I have a hard time paying attention to others when the subject matter doesn't interest me.	**T**	**F**
Sometimes, I find myself "tuning out" at business meetings, family gatherings, and social events.	**T**	**F**
I frequently find myself interrupting others to clarify points of discussion.	**T**	**F**
I can often anticipate what people are going to say—and I say it first.	**T**	**F**
When I participate in a discussion, I feel responsible for how well it's going.	**T**	**F**
I can tell by people's reactions that they're probably grateful I've finished their thoughts for them.	**T**	**F**
I can tell by the look on people's faces that they're probably annoyed when I interrupt them.	**T**	**F**

Think about your responses. Circle any of the statements that relate to something you'd like to change. Write a few lines about the changes you'd like to make for each one.

_____

_____

_____

_____

_____

_____

_____

_____

_____

8.

Do Something Nice for Someone Else—
and Don't Tell *Anyone* About It

While many of us frequently do nice things for others, we are almost certain to mention our acts of kindness to someone else, secretly seeking their approval. But there is something even more magical about doing something thoughtful and mentioning it to no one. By keeping your act to yourself, you ensure that the rewards truly come from the act of giving!

Think of something nice that you did for someone else. Make a list of the pros and cons of mentioning your act of kindness to another person. Then list the pros and cons of keeping your kindness to yourself. Which way works best for you and why?

Dear Diary,
I did something nice for someone today!
Here's what happened: _____

_____

_____

Here's what I did: _____

_____

_____

Dear Diary,
I told someone about my act of kindness.
Here's why: _____

_____

_____

Here's how I feel now that I've mentioned it:

On the plus side: *On the minus side:*

Dear Diary,
I've told no one about my act of kindness.
Here's why: _____
_____
_____

Here's how I feel about keeping it to myself:

On the plus side: *On the minus side:*

Look over your lists of pros and cons. Which way works best for you—telling or not telling someone about something nice you did for someone else? Why?

9.

Let Others Have the Glory

Our need for excessive attention comes from that ego-centered part of us that says, "Look at me. I'm special. My story is more interesting than yours." Although it's a difficult habit to break, surrendering your need for attention allows others to feel more relaxed around you. You, too, will feel more relaxed because you won't be waiting for your turn.

Can you let others have the glory? Complete this inventory to find out. Statements are presented in sets of three. Each one has a point value. Read all three statements and decide which one best describes your situation. Then write the point value in the space beside that statement.

1. As someone describes a wonderful trip he or she has just taken, I
____ listen and exclaim with enthusiasm, encouraging the speaker to tell more. (3)
____ listen politely, but inside I know that the trips I've taken were better. (2)
____ listen for a while, then interrupt to tell everyone about a trip I recently took. (1)

2. Friends are discussing a recent best-seller. I
____ exclaim that I could have written a better book. (1)
____ eagerly share my own thoughts about the book. (3)
____ talk about a different book that I have read. (2)

3. Friends I've recently made are describing a sport they played in high school. I
____ explain how difficult it was to compete with the athletes in my town. (2)
____ change the subject; I was always awful at sports. (1)
____ listen and share my own experiences to add to the conversation. (3)

4. A coworker is being complimented on a new pair of shoes. I
____ also exclaim how much I like them. (3)
____ keep quiet because I really don't like them. (2)
____ ask everyone to look at my shoes because I think they are nicer. (1)

5. Family members tell about items they bought at a holiday sale. I compare my skill and

___ exaggerate how much money I saved. (1)

___ ask if they checked out a store where I found a lot of bargains. (2)

___ good-naturedly share my experiences. (3)

6. Coworkers are talking about a new movie that just opened. I

___ join in the excitement of the movie. (3)

___ make sure everyone knows I've already seen it. (2)

___ tell the surprise ending. (1)

7. Parents are sharing humorous anecdotes about their children. I

___ point out why my child is special. (2)

___ make my child sound like the next Nobel Prize winner; I am proud. (1)

___ describe something funny my child did. (3)

8. On a warm summer night, neighbors are lamenting over their jobs. I

___ explain that I want to start my own business. (2)

___ commiserate and share my own experiences. (3)

___ describe my boss as a demon monster from another planet. (1)

9. A friend decides to go on a new fad diet. I

___ ask questions about the diet because it may be right for me. (3)

___ recount an article I recently read about the diet. (2)

___ share my own experiences with fad diets. (1)

10. A friend, upset with a family member, tells me the problem. I

___ exaggerate about someone in my family so the problem doesn't look so big. (2)

___ claim I don't know what my friend is going through. (1)

___ invite my friend to unload the problem as I listen and ask questions. (3)

Score: 21–30, you let others have the glory; 11–20, you still need some work in letting others have the glory; 1–10, you like the spotlight shining on you! Try to take a step back and enjoy the glory as others share their accomplishments.

10.

Learn to Live in the Present Moment

To a large degree, the measure of our peace of mind is determined by how much we are able to live in the present moment. When we allow past problems and future concerns to dominate our present moments, we end up anxious, frustrated, depressed, and hopeless. We also postpone our gratification, our stated priorities, and our happiness, often convincing ourselves that "someday" will be better than today.

Do you keep your attention on the here and now? If not, try the following.

1. First, realize that in order to cherish the now, we must make peace with the past. List those things that you've done or said in the past that you still regret today. Also include regrettable things that others have said or done to you that still sting.

Study the items on your list. Written down, they don't look so terrible, do they? Be aware that each item is history. Resolve today to put each of these regrets behind you.

2. Now make a list of what worries you about the future. What are you afraid of ?

3. How much time do you spend worrying about problems that never come to pass? Think back to some of the recent, looming concerns that evaporated before your eyes. Name one.

4. What kinds of troubles tend to occupy your mind? Check the categories that apply.

____ Financial
____ Relationships
____ Career
____ Family
____ Health
____ Other _____

Circle the items on this list that you really do have control over. Chances are you've circled very few of them. But chances are you've let them have a lot of control over you.

5. Now, list those things you've been putting off until "someday," whether it's cleaning out the closet or taking a trip.
Circle the items on this list that you can accomplish today.

Take a look at those longer-term projects on your list, the ones that you haven't started because you're afraid you'll be unable to complete them. Guess what? You're right—if you don't start them, you *won't* finish them. Now's the time to begin.

Write down one of the long-term projects from your list and start working on it. Understand that we can only control the present, but by the same token, our future begins right now. So act! And remember, you can always change your mind later.

Once you've unshackled yourself from the past and stopped worrying about the future, you'll find yourself living and acting in the present.

11.

Imagine That Everyone Is Enlightened Except You

Imagine that the people you meet are all perfectly enlightened—they're here to teach you something. Your job is to try to determine what the people in your life are trying to teach you. You'll find that if you do this, you'll be far less annoyed, bothered, and frustrated by the actions and imperfections of other people.

Are you prepared to change your perceptions from "Why are they doing this?" to "What are they trying to teach me?" If so, try to think of something you can learn from each of the following people in your life and write it in the blank.

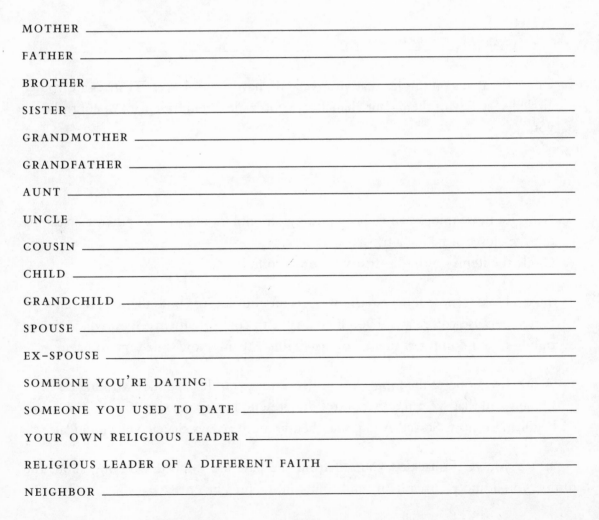

MOTHER _____

FATHER _____

BROTHER _____

SISTER _____

GRANDMOTHER _____

GRANDFATHER _____

AUNT _____

UNCLE _____

COUSIN _____

CHILD _____

GRANDCHILD _____

SPOUSE _____

EX-SPOUSE _____

SOMEONE YOU'RE DATING _____

SOMEONE YOU USED TO DATE _____

YOUR OWN RELIGIOUS LEADER _____

RELIGIOUS LEADER OF A DIFFERENT FAITH _____

NEIGHBOR _____

TEACHER _____

COACH _____

FRIEND (AS A CHILD) _____

FRIEND (AS A GROWN-UP) _____

CLASSMATE YOU DISLIKED _____

SOMEONE WHO BEAT YOU UP _____

A PARENT'S FRIEND _____

DOCTOR _____

STORE CLERK _____

DELIVERY PERSON _____

POLICE OFFICER _____

REPAIR PERSON _____

TELEPHONE SALESPERSON _____

PANHANDLER _____

BOSS _____

POLITICIAN _____

ENTERTAINER (YOU DON'T PERSONALLY KNOW) _____

Score: Cross out any people who have never been in your life. For each person you can recall teaching you a life lesson, score 1. Then divide your score by the total number of people left to get a percentage. If you scored below 50%, you have a lot to learn; 50%–75%, you pay some attention; 75%–90%, you're open-minded; above 90%, you're a good listener.

12.

Let Others Be "Right" Most of the Time

Many people believe that it's somehow their job to show others how their positions are incorrect. Think about it. Has anyone you know ever thanked you when you corrected them or made yourself "right" at their expense? Of course not. All of us hate to be corrected. We all want our positions to be respected and understood by others. Being listened to and heard is one of the greatest desires of the human heart. And those who learn to listen are the most loved and respected.

Can you allow others the joy of being "right"? Complete this inventory to find out. Read all three statements and decide which one best describes your situation. Then write the point value in the space beside that statement.

1. A friend is describing a new piece of home gym equipment recently purchased. I
___ immediately explain why it won't work; after all, I'm just being helpful. (1)
___ explain why my gym equipment is better. (2)
___ listen with interest and ask questions about it. (3)

2. Neighbors are discussing why the home team recently lost a game. I
___ agree with their opinions and suggest some of my own. (3)
___ loudly proclaim that my reasoning is the right one. (1)
___ argue until my point wins. (2)

3. When someone finds fault with a movie I really enjoy, I
___ cut them off and tell them that they didn't get the point. (1)
___ rationally assert my point of view. (2)
___ listen and calmly consider what they have to say. (3)

4. I disagree with a coworker on the status of a project. I
___ declare my coworker to be totally off base and explain why. (1)
___ listen with an open mind and agree with some of my coworker's points. (3)
___ calmly point out why my coworker is wrong, then explain why. (2)

5. A friend remembers an event we both shared in the past differently than I do. I
___ try to see the story from my friend's point of view. (3)
___ tell my friend that he or she is totally mistaken; it did not happen that way. (1)
___ point out why my version of the event might be more accurate. (2)

6. A sibling has learned about a new type of cold medicine. I
___ won't even listen; my medicine works best for me. (1)
___ pretend to listen but know I won't try it. (2)
___ listen with an open mind, for I might learn something. (3)

7. A colleague has an idea, but it goes against a plan I am about to suggest. I
___ reevaluate my plan in light of my colleague's ideas. (3)
___ take into account my colleague's ideas but hold firm to my own. (2)
___ tell everyone that my idea is much more efficient than my colleague's. (1)

8. My friends and I are discussing the greatest novel ever written. I
___ listen objectively and ask questions about my friends' choices. (3)
___ talk loudly to get my point across. (2)
___ shake my head at the stupidity of my friends' ideas, but offer none of my own. (1)

9. A new person at work has an idea for how to get along with a difficult boss. I
___ might listen but probably won't take the advice. (2)
___ won't listen—after all, I have more experience with my boss. (1)
___ listen objectively, thinking someone new might have a fresh approach. (3)

10. A friend talks about a wildlife documentary recently shown on television. I
___ encourage my friend to tell me more. (3)
___ listen, then explain what I know about the subject. (2)
___ complain that the documentary sounds fictitious. (1)

Score: 21–30, you tend to let others be "right." 11–20, half right! Try to listen more before you speak your mind. 1–10, you think you are right more often than not. Practice opening your mind to what others have to say—you just might find that they're right sometimes, too.

13.

Become More Patient

The quality of patience goes a long way toward creating a more peaceful and loving self. Becoming more patient involves opening your heart to the present moment, even if you don't like it. Patience also involves seeing the innocence in others, adding a dimension of ease and acceptance to your life.

Are you patient? Answer this questionnaire to find out. If your answer to a question is **never**, circle 0; for **sometimes**, circle 1; for **often**, circle 2; for **always**, circle 3.

1.	While driving, I weave in and out of traffic.	0	1	2	3
2.	When I'm in a traffic jam, I curse.	0	1	2	3
3.	When my train is late arriving at my station, I pace up and down the platform.	0	1	2	3
4.	When the train or plane in which I'm riding is late to my destination, I keep looking at my watch.	0	1	2	3
5.	I get angry when a person I'm meeting is late.	0	1	2	3
6.	When I'm late for an appointment, I become very agitated.	0	1	2	3
7.	I get angry when a meeting starts late.	0	1	2	3
8.	I get angry when I try to explain something and the other person doesn't understand.	0	1	2	3
9.	I get angry when someone eats something I've been saving for myself.	0	1	2	3
10.	I get angry at myself when I can't remember something.	0	1	2	3
11.	I wish I were moving faster in my career.	0	1	2	3
12.	I get annoyed when someone interrupts me while I'm working.	0	1	2	3

13. I get annoyed when someone calls me while I'm watching television. 0

14. I can't stand stupid questions. 0

15. I can't stand when people talk softly. 0

16. I can't stand when people talk slowly. 0

17. I can't stand when people think they're correcting me—and they're wrong. 0

18. I hate waiting in line. 0

19. I hate when I pick the shortest line and it turns out to take the longest. 0

20. I hang up the phone if I get put on hold. 0

21. I fume if a service person arrives late. 0

22. I feel anxious if something takes longer than I thought it would. 0

23. I feel that things that take a long time are not worth doing. (

24. I can't wait to see what will happen next. (

25. I can't help telling secrets. (

Score: If you've scored more than 60, you'd better check your ately; 40–59, you're a candidate for stress reduction; 25–39, 13–24, you're really laid back; 12 or less, you're a candidate for

14.

Create "Patience Practice Periods"

is a quality of heart that can be greatly enhanced with practice. Whether you
deal with children, your boss, or a difficult person or situation—if you don't
'sweat the small stuff," improving your patience is a great way to start.
fective way to improve your own patience is to create actual practice periods.
periods of time that you set up in your mind to practice the art of patience.
ollowing.

impatient are you? Check all that apply:
d to drive above the speed limit.
smashed or thrown away a tool or appliance I couldn't figure out how to use.
e to wait on line, even a short line.
ver read instructions.
he phone, I get furious when I have to deal with an automated voice
ucting me to press a series of numbers.
en feel that when people ask me to explain something, they ask stupid
tions.
ie mall, people walk too slowly and get in my way.

checked more than half of these, you need to practice being more patient—
rself and with others.

a list of times you've lost your patience with others. What were the
nstances?

frequently do you lose your patience? How do you express you impatience?

4. Are you more impatient with strangers or with people you know?

5. Imagine yourself in each of the circumstances you listed under question 2—only this time, you don't lose your patience. Write down how different you feel and how others respond differently to you.

6. Imagine yourself in a slow-moving checkout line at a grocery store. Make a list of things you can do to practice your patience.

7. Imagine yourself deep in thought at work. Then someone comes in and interrupts you. Make a list of things you can do to keep your cool and preserve your patience.

8. Imagine yourself in your car. Traffic is slow and driving is tricky. Make a list of things you can do to remain courteous and maintain your patience.

Remember: If you find yourself losing patience, step away from what you're doing for a few minutes and come back to it.

15.

Be the First One to Act Loving or Reach Out

So many of us hold on to little resentments. Stubbornly, we wait for someone else to reach out to us. Whenever we hold on to our anger, we turn "small stuff" into "big stuff" in our minds. We start to believe that our positions are more important than our happiness. They are not. The way to be happy is to let go and reach out. Let other people be right. They, in turn, will become less defensive and more loving toward you. They might even reach back!

Are you too stubborn—or too scared—to reach out first? Complete this inventory to find out. Read all three statements and decide which one best describes your situation. Then write the point value in the space beside that statement.

1.

____ I never send out a holiday card until I receive one first. (1)

____ I sometimes send out holiday cards without waiting to see who sends me one. (2)

____ I send out holiday cards to everyone, whether or not they send one back to me. (3)

2.

____ I would never contact the spouse of a divorced friend. (1)

____ I would contact the spouse of a divorced friend; he or she was my friend, too. (3)

____ I might contact the spouse of a divorced friend. (2)

3.

____ I'd forgive my best friend for dating an ex-boyfriend or ex-girlfriend, but I wouldn't forget it. (2)

____ I'd *never* forgive my best friend for dating an ex-boyfriend or ex-girlfriend. (1)

____ I'd forgive my best friend for dating an ex-boyfriend or ex-girlfriend. (3)

4.

____ I might invite a friend to a party even though I'd not been invited to theirs. (2)

____ I would invite a friend to a party, even though I'd not been invited to theirs; they probably had their reasons. (3)

____ I would never invite a friend to a party if I had not been invited to theirs. (1)

5.

____ I would apologize to a coworker for an argument during a meeting. (3)

____ I would never apologize to a coworker for an argument during a meeting. (1)

____ I might apologize to a coworker for an argument during a meeting. (2)

6.

____ If a friend has been too busy to return a call, I might call again. (2)

____ If a friend has been too busy to return a call, I would never call again. (1)

____ If a friend has been too busy, I would definitely call again. (3)

7.

____ I would definitely say I was sorry if my spouse and I had a fight, no matter who was right or wrong. (3)

____ I might say I was sorry if my spouse and I had a fight; it depends what the fight was about. (2)

____ I would never say I was sorry if my spouse and I had a fight, no matter who was right or wrong. (1)

8.

____ I would never forgive someone for embarrassing me in public. (1)

____ I would tell someone not to worry about having embarrassed me if it was clear that he or she didn't mean it. (3)

____ I might forgive someone for embarrassing me, depending upon the situation. (2)

9.

____ If my best friend arranged a bad blind date, I might not call for a while. (2)

____ If my best friend arranged a bad blind date, I would immediately call to have a good laugh. (3)

____ If my best friend arranged a bad blind date, I would never call my friend again. (1)

10.

____ I would call a friend to ask how a new date went, even though he or she had canceled plans we'd made. (3)

—— I might call a friend to ask how a new date went, even though he or she had canceled plans we'd made. (2)

—— I would never call a friend to ask how a new date went if he or she had canceled plans we'd made. (1)

Score: 21–30, you tend to be the first one to reach out in a loving way; 11–20, try harder to extend that olive branch; 1–10, you have a hard time letting go of old wounds. Take the first step by calling someone you haven't spoken to in a while. See how much better you feel!

16.

Ask Yourself the Question, "Will This Matter a Year from Now?"

Imagine that whatever circumstance you are dealing with isn't happening right now, but a year from now. Then simply ask yourself, "Is this situation really as important as I'm making it out to be?" Once in a great while it may be—but a vast majority of the time, it simply isn't. While this simple game won't solve all your problems, it can give you an enormous amount of perspective.

Do you use up lots of energy feeling angry and overwhelmed about things that won't matter a year from now? If so, try the following.

1. Check all that apply:
I can recall:
____ what I had for lunch yesterday.

____ what I wore last Monday.

____ the last movie I saw.

____ what my last argument was about.

____ the last time a cold made me feel miserable.

____ the last time I overpaid for something.

____ the last time I was publicly embarrassed.

____ the last time I made a costly mistake.

2. When they were happening, how much time and effort did you spend making the decisions or worrying about the situations above? How important are they to you now?

3. In the left-hand column below, make a list of situations that troubled you last year. In the right-hand column, list the long-term effects of each situation. Are you able to see that the problems that once loomed so large now don't seem so troublesome?

WHAT I WORRIED ABOUT A YEAR AGO	WHAT THE CONSEQUENCES ARE TODAY

At work

At home

With relationships

About my future

4. Now, make a list of the troubles you're facing today, and imagine where they'll be a year from now.

MY WORRIES TODAY	HOW THEY'LL MATTER NEXT YEAR
At work	
At home	
With relationships	
About my future	

17.

Surrender to the Fact That Life Isn't Fair

One of the nice things about surrendering to the fact that life isn't fair is that it keeps us from feeling sorry for ourselves by encouraging us to do the very best we can with what we have. It also keeps us from feeling sorry for others because we are reminded that everyone is dealt a different hand, and everyone has unique strengths and challenges.

Do you often find yourself thinking about the injustices of the world? The true/false exercise below will help you isolate problem areas.

Some people are "luckier" than others.	T	F
It's human nature to compare one's lot in life with another person's.	T	F
Even people who have suffered great loss or tragedy can be happy.	T	F
Even people who have wealth, fame, and privilege can be miserable.	T	F
A person's attitude about the world is his or her greatest asset.	T	F
Everyone has the power to change his or her attitude about the world.	T	F
Life is hard for everyone, regardless of circumstances.	T	F
Even if life isn't fair, everyone has the same chance to be happy.	T	F
It's human nature to always want more than we have.	T	F
The world's always picking on me.	T	F

1. List ten things you feel fortunate that life has given you.

2. List ten things you wish you didn't have to deal with in your life, but have successfully compensated for.

3. Write the name of someone who you feel has been unfairly treated by life.

   What do you admire about this person?

4. Write the name of someone who you feel leads an especially "charmed" life.

   Would you trade your life for his or hers? List your reasons why or why not.

5. If you could change one thing in your life, what would it be?

   Why would you change it?

18.

Allow Yourself to Be Bored

For many of us, it's almost impossible to sit still and do nothing, much less relax. But occasional boredom can actually be good! By allowing ourselves to be bored, even for an hour or less, we can replace our feelings of boredom with feelings of peace. The beauty of doing nothing is that it teaches you to clear your mind and relax. Just like your body, your mind needs an occasional break from its hectic routine.

Do you allow yourself to be bored? Complete this inventory to find out. Read all three statements and decide which one best describes your situation. Then write the point value in the space beside that statement.

1. While watching television, I
—— always change the channel during commercials. (2)
—— do the crossword puzzle during commercials. (1)
—— let my mind wander during commercials. (3)

2. When I have a few minutes to spare before going to a meeting, I
—— clear my mind and try to become totally calm and relaxed. (3)
—— go over my notes to make sure I haven't missed anything. (2)
—— try to do twelve things at once! (1)

3. While waiting for a plane at the airport, I might
—— begin a new book. (2)
—— close my eyes and relax before my flight. (3)
—— think about all the things I have to do once I get to where I'm going. (1)

4. I have a few minutes before the guests arrive for my party. I
—— try to squeeze in a load of laundry. (1)
—— check to be sure everything is ready. (2)
—— relax and take a deep breath. (3)

5. My best friend suddenly cancels our Friday night plans. I
—— quickly call everyone I know to find something else to do. (1)

___ decide to rent that video I've been meaning to watch. (2)

___ take a bubble bath. (3)

6. A baseball game I'm about to attend is postponed due to rain. I

___ decide this is a good time to check out that new sports center. (1)

___ sit back in my recliner and relax. (3)

___ flip the channels on my TV to see if there's another game to watch. (2)

7. The doctor is running behind schedule. I

___ leave and come back later; I have errands to run. (1)

___ flip through the magazines in the waiting room. (2)

___ take advantage of the few minutes of free time and do nothing. (3)

8. I have finished tidying up the house. I

___ feel inclined to straighten up a bit more. (2)

___ leisurely sip a cup of tea. (3)

___ plan what to make for dinner. (1)

9. A coworker needs to cancel a lunch date. I

___ close my office door and unwind. (3)

___ try to get caught up on my work. (1)

___ call someone else to go out to lunch with me. (2)

10. My car pool partner is late due to traffic. I

___ read the morning paper. (2)

___ get a head start on my work. (1)

___ have another cup of coffee. (3)

Score: 21–30, you are able to let yourself be bored; 11–20, you're able to relax sometimes, but are anxious at other times; 1–10, you have a problem relaxing. Try being bored instead of filling up all your time.

19.

Lower Your Tolerance to Stress

Look around you. You'll notice that people who say, "I can handle lots of stress" will *always* be under a great deal of it! Usually it takes a crisis of some kind to wake up a stressed-out person. What you want to start doing is noticing your stress early, while it's manageable and easy to control.

Do you want to lower your tolerance to stress? Take this stress test and see what your problem areas are. Circle 0 for **never**, 1 for **sometimes**, 2 for **often**, and 3 for **always**. Then go back and check off the questions for which you circled a 2 or a 3. Try to come up with strategies for lowering your tolerance to stress in those areas.

1. I wish I could get more work done than I do now.   0   1   2   3

2. I wish I could get by on less sleep.   0   1   2   3

3. Having to stop work for meals is a drag.   0   1   2   3

4. I don't have time for everything I want to do.   0   1   2   3

5. I have so many things to do, I don't know what to do first.   0   1   2   3

6. Finding time for family and friends gets harder all the time.   0   1   2   3

7. When I have free time, all I can think of is work.   0   1   2   3

8. I can't relax.   0   1   2   3

9. I must find a way to make more money—soon.   0   1   2   3

10. People expect too much of me.   0   1   2   3

11. I don't know how I'll measure up.   0   1   2   3

12. I wish I could do better than I'm doing.   0   1   2   3

13. I'm worried about my future.   0   1   2   3

14. I have so many problems that I don't know what to do.   0   1   2   3

15. I wish I could solve all my problems.   0   1   2   3

16. I wish I knew what I was meant to do with my life.   0   1   2   3

Which of the following stress warning signs have you experienced? Put a check mark next to each one. Try to notice when you feel one of the stress signs. Think how you might change your behavior. Write it in the blank provided.

FREQUENT HEADACHES _____

MUSCLE TENSION OR SPASMS _____

STOMACH PROBLEMS _____

EXCESSIVE SWEATING _____

RAPID OR POUNDING HEARTBEAT _____

ALLERGIES _____

FREQUENT ILLNESS _____

INSOMNIA _____

FATIGUE _____

ANXIETY _____

DEPRESSION _____

FEELING OF BEING OVERWHELMED _____

HYPERACTIVITY _____

FREQUENT TEMPER _____

CONFUSION OR FORGETFULNESS _____

RESTLESSNESS OR LACK OF CONCENTRATION _____

WEIGHT CHANGE _____

OBSESSIVE OR COMPULSIVE BEHAVIOR _____

DRUG USE (INCLUDING ALCOHOL AND TOBACCO) _____

WORRY OR FEARFULNESS _____

20.

Once a Week, Write a Heartfelt Letter

Chances are, there are a number of people in your life who are quite deserving of a friendly, heartfelt letter. The purpose of your letter is very simple: to express love and gratitude. Not only does writing and sending a note like this focus your attention on what's right in your life, but the person receiving it will, in all likelihood, be extremely touched and grateful.

Think of someone you'd like to write to. Then write a practice letter below. You'll be glad you did!

(Date) _____

Dear _____,

I woke up this morning thinking of how lucky I am to have people like you in my life.

_____

_____

_____

_____

Thank you so much for being my friend. I am truly blessed, and wish _____ for you.

Love,

21.

Imagine Yourself at Your Own Funeral

Almost universally, when people look back on their lives, they wish that their priorities had been different. With few exceptions, people wish they hadn't "sweated the small stuff" so much. Instead, they wish they had spent more time with the people and activities that they truly loved.

Imagining yourself at your own funeral allows you to look back at your life while you still have the chance to make some important changes. Consider your own death and, in the process, your life. Your answers to these questions will help you gain perspective.

1. If you imagine you died of anything but old age, what do you think killed you?

2. Imagine you're floating above the cemetery, looking down at the people attending your funeral. Are there any old friends, colleagues, or relatives with whom you've lost touch, whom you meant to see while you were alive? Make a list of whom you see that you'd like to speak with.

3. If you could hear the private thoughts of these people, what would they be thinking about you? Write their thoughts next to their names.

4. Everyone who cares for you is assembled at your funeral. If you could leave them with one thought, what would it be? Write it here.

5. Let's say your worst enemy showed up at your funeral. What thought would you leave for him or her, if you could? Write it here.

6. Make a list of things you would regret leaving behind or leaving unfinished.

7. Make a list of your most cherished accomplishments.

8. What do you think you would be most remembered for?

9. Write your eulogy here.

22.

Repeat to Yourself, "Life Isn't an Emergency"

Although most people believe otherwise, life *isn't* an emergency. We take our own goals so seriously that we forget to have fun along the way, and we forget to cut ourselves some slack. Life will usually go on if things don't go according to plan. Keep reminding yourself, "Life isn't an emergency."

Do you tend to create your own emergencies? Complete this inventory to find out. Read all three statements and decide which one best describes your situation. Then write the point value in the space beside that statement.

1.
___ Getting stuck in traffic is the worst thing that could happen to me. (1)
___ Sometimes getting stuck in traffic really bothers me. (2)
___ There's nothing I can do about traffic, so I don't let it bother me. (3)

2.
___ I make sure to finish reading library books so I can return them on time. (1)
___ It's okay if I don't finish a book by its due date; I'll check it out again. (3)
___ I usually try to finish reading a library book before it's due back. (2)

3.
___ I occasionally panic if I feel I have too much work to do. (2)
___ I never panic if I feel I have too much work to do; it will get done somehow. (3)
___ I always panic if I feel I have too much work to do; it will never get done. (1)

4.
___ I seldom worry about the April 15 tax deadline; I can file an extension. (3)
___ I sometimes worry about paying my taxes by April 15. (2)
___ I always worry about April 15; it feels like the end of the world. (1)

5. If the washing machine were to break down, I would
___ feel so frustrated that I wouldn't know what to do. (1)

___ call the repair person and do something else with my time. (3)

___ take my laundry to the laundromat. (2)

6. If my spouse brought a coworker home for dinner unexpectedly, I would

___ set an extra plate. (3)

___ smile, but tell my spouse he or she was inconsiderate for not calling first. (2)

___ leave and let my spouse cook dinner. (1)

7. Taking a pet to the vet for an emergency means I must put off finishing a project. I

___ get extremely upset thinking I'll never finish the project. (1)

___ plan the rest of my time so I can finish the project. (2)

___ don't worry; it will be finished when I have time. (3)

8. Once again, I find myself shopping for holiday presents at the last minute. I

___ feel annoyed with myself, but grudgingly go to the mall. (2)

___ shrug my shoulders and get ready to head to the mall in the holiday spirit. (3)

___ have a panic attack; I hate the mall at holiday time. (1)

9. My in-laws just called from the airport unexpectedly, and my spouse has gone to pick them up. I

___ run around the house, frantically trying to clean. (1)

___ tidy things up, wishing they had called sooner. (2)

___ straighten up what I can. (3)

10. I only have a one-hour window to take care of personal errands each day. I

___ spread my errands out over the week. (3)

___ try to do everything at once. (1)

___ always complain about not having enough time, but somehow get everything done. (2)

Score: 21–30, you realize that many of the problems we face each day are just a part of life; 11–20, try a bit harder to reevaluate those "emergencies" to make them less significant; 1–10, you tend to see *everything* as an emergency. Try to reevaluate each instance in the scheme of your life.

23.

Experiment with Your Back Burner

Using your back burner means allowing your mind to solve a problem while you are busy doing something else. The thoughts and ideas we feed the back burners of our minds must be left alone to simmer properly. The simple technique of gently holding a problem in your mind without actively analyzing it will greatly reduce the stress and effort in your life.

Do you use your back burner to solve problems? If not, try this exercise:

1. In a single sentence, write down what it is you're trying to solve or work out. Phrase it in terms of a goal, not a problem. Be sure to use lots of active words.

2. Make a list of ingredients you want to put on the back burner—thoughts that may help you to reach your goal. This is a brainstorming list of anything that may pop into your head while you're formulating your question. Some ingredients may not make any sense at first, but list them anyway. Your back burner has ways of making connections!

3. Make a more thoughtful list of the issues related to what you're trying to solve. For example, how will the solution relate to other people? To helping you? What will you achieve by finding an answer?

4. The best time for your back burner to work is while your front burner is involved with something else. Look over what you've written above just before you begin a new book or prior to going off to a concert, play, or movie. While your conscious thoughts are focused, your back burner is simmering away. Be sure to read your sentence and lists right before you go to bed, too.

5. Write the one-sentence question on a three-by-five-inch card that you can carry with you and refer to throughout the day.

As you repeat this exercise with other challenges you want to commit to your back burner, you'll find that the steps become automatic. Eventually you'll need only to write down the question you hope to answer, and all the other steps will be done in your head.

24.

Spend a Moment Every Day Thinking of Someone to Thank

You probably have many people in your life you feel grateful for: friends, family members, people from your past, teachers, people from work, as well as countless others. Start your day thinking of someone to thank. What this exercise reminds you to do is to focus on the good in your life. If you wake up with gratitude on your mind, it's hard to feel anything but peace.

Do you take time each day to think of someone to thank? If not, get started with these thirty-nine reasons to be grateful. Fill in the appropriate name(s) of the person(s) who:

1. Helped me up when I fell. _____

2. Held me when I was afraid. _____

3. Held an umbrella over me. _____

4. Gave me hot cocoa to warm me up. _____

5. Sat through the night with me when I was sick. _____

6. Saved me from being late for school. _____

7. Introduced me to my favorite book. _____

8. Introduced me to my favorite movie. _____

9. Let me stay up late to watch a special TV show. _____

10. Took me to my first circus. _____

11. Didn't yell at me when I was learning to drive. _____

12. Took my feelings seriously. _____

13. Gave me just the present I wanted. _____

14. Came to see me from a great distance. _____

15. Remembered my birthday. _____

16. Renewed a friendship after many years. _____

17. Returned my lost wallet. _____

18. Studied all night with me. _____

19. Helped me get rid of a hangover. _____

20. Introduced me to the love of my life. _____

21. Helped me get over a broken heart. _____

22. Was kind to me when I needed a friend. _____

23. Talked me out of a bad investment. _____

24. Helped me to stop and smell the roses. _____

25. Taught me how to catch a baseball. _____

26. Taught me how to dance. _____

27. Showed me how to tie a necktie. _____

28. Told me the truth about the "birds and the bees." _____

29. Saved me from making a fool of myself. _____

30. Didn't laugh when I made a fool of myself. _____

31. Showed me how to plant seeds. _____

32. Gave me good advice. _____

33. Lent me money when I needed it. _____

34. Took me outside to look at the stars. _____

35. Helped me learn how to swim. _____

36. Gave me a surprise party. _____

37. Rehearsed lines with me for a play. _____

38. Rubbed my sore shoulders. _____

39. Baked cookies for me. _____

25.

Smile at Strangers, Look into Their Eyes, and Say Hello

Have you ever noticed how little eye contact most of us have with strangers? Why? Are we afraid of them? What keeps us from opening our hearts to people we don't know? Usually there is a parallel between our attitude toward strangers and our overall level of happiness.

Complete this inventory to find out about your attitude toward strangers—and, just maybe, yourself! Circle the word to the right as it applies to your situation.

1. I would ask a stranger for help if I needed it.   Never   Rarely   Sometimes   Often   Always

2. When a stranger stops me, I'm suspicious at first.   Never   Rarely   Sometimes   Often   Always

3. People perceive me as friendly.   Never   Rarely   Sometimes   Often   Always

4. Most people are friendly if given a chance.   Never   Rarely   Sometimes   Often   Always

5. Most people don't like to be approached by strangers.   Never   Rarely   Sometimes   Often   Always

6. When a stranger stops me, I resent the interruption at first.   Never   Rarely   Sometimes   Often   Always

7. I feel good after helping a stranger.   Never   Rarely   Sometimes   Often   Always

8. When I see a stranger who needs help, I offer my assistance.   Never   Rarely   Sometimes   Often   Always

9. I'm embarrassed when a stranger offers to help me.   Never   Rarely   Sometimes   Often   Always

10. I've been taken advantage of by a stranger I've tried to help.   Never   Rarely   Sometimes   Often   Always

11. I initiate conversations with clerks and waiters.	Never	Rarely	Sometimes	Often	Always
12. Frequent eye contact makes me uncomfortable.	Never	Rarely	Sometimes	Often	Always
13. I find it difficult to initiate eye contact.	Never	Rarely	Sometimes	Often	Always
14. I enjoy people who look me in the eye.	Never	Rarely	Sometimes	Often	Always
15. Compared to my friends, I'm shy.	Never	Rarely	Sometimes	Often	Always

1. Write a sentence that describes how you would like to change your behavior toward strangers. Start it with "I resolve to . . ."

2. List the benefits of changing your behavior toward strangers.

3. List the obstacles in your mind that are preventing you from relating to strangers in the way you'd like.

4. Circle the items on the above list that are based on your experience with strangers. If some of the obstacles on your list aren't based on your experience, where do you think those attitudes came from? Make the decision to put those thoughts to rest.

26.

Set Aside Quiet Time, Every Day

There is something rejuvenating and peaceful about being alone and having some time to reflect, work, or simply enjoy the quiet. Whether it's ten minutes of meditation or yoga, spending a little time in nature, or locking the bathroom door and taking a ten-minute bath, quiet time to yourself is a vital part of life.

Do you set aside some time for yourself every day? If not, then consider the following.

1. Think about your favorite time of the day. How do you use this time?

2. Think about your favorite activities. List at least a dozen things you like to do. Circle the ones that balance the noise and confusion of everyday life.

3. Think about how you spend your time. List the major events of each day. How much time do you give to each one?

4. Think about the time that is left. Draw a circle and divide it into six parts: *friends, family, work, play, sleep, quiet time.* Your pie will not be evenly cut! What slice of the pie is left for quiet time?

5. Now think about your own worst habits. Do they take time away from creating your own inner peace? Resolve to change that. Establish your own five-point plan:

Choose a time.

Choose a place.

Choose something you like to do in complete solitude.

Find a way to do it.

Make a date with yourself—same time, same place, every day!

27.

Imagine the People in Your Life as Tiny Infants
and as One-Hundred-Year-Old Adults

Think of someone who truly irritates you, who makes you feel angry. Close your eyes and try to imagine this person as a tiny infant. Now, roll forward the clock one hundred years. See the same person as a very old adult. Know that each of us, no matter what stage of life, makes or has made mistakes. Playing with this technique provides both perspective and compassion.

Can you imagine the people in your life as tiny infants and as one-hundred-year-old adults? If not, then try this simple exercise.

1. Think of someone who irritates you or makes you feel angry. Imagine that person as he or she looks in the present. Describe him or her.

2. Think of specific instances when he or she has made you feel annoyed or angry. List the qualities that most disturb you about that individual.

3. Now roll back the clock a few decades. Imagine that same person as an infant. Describe him or her.

4. Think of the qualities that make a baby especially vulnerable. List those qualities below. (Keep in mind that your nemesis is that baby!)

5. Now roll the clock ahead a few decades. Imagine that same person as a very elderly adult. Describe him or her.

6. Think of the qualities that make an elderly person especially vulnerable. List those qualities below. (Keep in mind that your nemesis is now one hundred years old!)

7. Do these new perspectives on this person help open your heart to greater compassion? Why or why not?

8. Think about how you can put this strategy into practice the next time you're confronted with behavior that either frustrates or angers you. List ten times when you would use this and on whom.

28.

Seek First to Understand

When you understand where people are coming from, what they are trying to say, and what's important to them, *being* understood flows naturally; it falls into place with virtually no effort. When you reverse this position, the effort you exert will be felt by you and the people you are trying to reach. Seeking first to understand isn't about who's right or wrong; it is a philosophy of effective communication.

How open are you to understanding where people are coming from? Take this questionnaire to find out. Answer **yes**, **sometimes**, or **no** to each of the questions.

1. I believe that people much younger than I am have little to offer me in conversations.

2. I believe that people much older than I am have little to offer me in conversations.

3. At a gathering I try to avoid people who are physically different from me.

4. At a gathering I try to avoid people who I believe are not physically attractive.

5. At a gathering I try to avoid people who are tastelessly dressed.

6. I avoid listening to people whose speech patterns annoy me.

7. I avoid talking with anyone whose voice annoys me.

8. I avoid meeting people who apparently belong to an ethnic group other than my own.

9. People whose occupation is quite different from mine can't possibly understand my work or have anything worthwhile to say about it.

10. I prefer to talk with people who live near me.

11. I prefer to talk with people who have a lot of money.

12. When I am talking with someone I've just met, I hesitate to ask a lot of questions.

13. When I am talking with someone I've just met, I prefer to talk about myself first.

14. If I am an expert in a subject, I can't learn anything from an amateur.

15. I can't learn anything about my religion from someone who doesn't practice it.

16. A person who hasn't shared an experience with me can't possibly have anything enlightening to say about it.

17. If someone is telling a story about an experience similar to mine, I can't wait to tell my own story.

18. If someone interrupts me, I get very upset.

19. At a gathering I like to be the center of attention by dominating the conversation.

20. My opinion counts more than anyone else's.

21. At work it's very important for everyone to know up front where I stand on an issue.

22. I often think I know what a person is going to say before he or she says it.

23. When I'm making a presentation at work, I prefer that nobody disagrees with me.

24. If I give someone an assignment, I always like having it done my way.

25. Giving people a chance to offer a different explanation for something that seems obvious is a waste of time.

26. Listening to someone with an opposing political view is pointless.

27. When someone is telling a story and says something I know to be wrong, I interrupt with the correct version.

28. When someone voices an opinion different from my own, I try to shut that person up.

29. When everyone else seems to understand what a speaker is saying, it is better to pretend to understand than risk embarrassment by asking questions.

30. It's better to assume I know what a person's stand on an issue is than to risk embarrassment by asking the person.

Score: The more you answered *yes* or *sometimes*, the more you must seek to understand.

29.

Become a Better Listener

Are you content to listen to the *entire* thought of someone rather than waiting impatiently for your chance to respond? If so, then you are an effective listener.

Check your listening skills below. This true/false exercise will help you isolate your problem areas.

I'm not good at following verbal travel directions.	**T**	**F**
Before responding to what someone has told me, I restate in my own words what they said.	**T**	**F**
I forget people's names almost as soon as I learn them.	**T**	**F**
Most people equate slow responses to questions with slow thinking.	**T**	**F**
I doodle or fidget when on the phone.	**T**	**F**
In conversations, I pause before responding.	**T**	**F**
People find me easy to talk to.	**T**	**F**
People ask for my advice.	**T**	**F**
In conversation, I ask a lot of questions.	**T**	**F**
While someone is talking to me, I'm mentally preparing my response before they're finished.	**T**	**F**

1. Think about the best listener you know. List the qualities that make him or her a good listener.

Circle the qualities you share with this person. Concentrate on improving upon the qualities you left uncircled.

2. Think about the worst listener you know. List the behaviors that make it clear this person isn't hearing what you're saying.

Circle the qualities you share with this person. Work on eliminating these habits from your own listening.

3. List how better listening skills will help you in these situations.
   At work:

   In your relationships:

   In social situations:

30.

Choose Your Battles Wisely

"Choose your battles wisely" is a popular phrase in parenting, but is equally important in living a contented life. It suggests that life is filled with opportunities to choose between making a big deal out of something or simply letting it go, realizing it doesn't really matter. If you choose your battles wisely, you'll be far more effective in winning those that are truly important.

Do you "choose your battles wisely"? Complete this inventory to find out. Statements are presented in sets of three. Each one has a point value. Read all three statements and decide which one best describes your situation. Then write the point value in the space beside that statement.

1.
____ I frequently argue with friends about which restaurant or movie to go to. (1)
____ I sometimes argue with friends about which restaurant or movie to go to. (2)
____ An evening out is seldom a source of argument for me. (3)

2. When my neighbors are noisy,
____ I ignore it. (3)
____ I politely ask them to be quiet. (2)
____ I call the police. (1)

3.
____ I always react to someone's mistake, no matter how small it may be. (1)
____ I sometimes react to minor mistakes. (2)
____ I rarely take the time to react to someone's minor mistake. (3)

4. If a stranger cuts me off while I'm driving,
____ I just shrug and drive away. (3)
____ I usually mutter under my breath. (2)
____ I drive beside the car and start to scream. (1)

5.

___ I often argue with my family about how much time it takes to get someplace. (1)

___ I sometimes argue with my family about allowing enough time to get to a place. (2)

___ I rarely argue with my family about any short-term travel plans. (3)

6.

___ I always have to have the last word. (1)

___ I am willing to listen but still like to have the last word. (2)

___ I listen with an open mind. (3)

7.

___ I expect that people will disagree with me from time to time. (3)

___ Sometimes it bothers me when people don't see things my way. (2)

___ I get angry when people don't agree with me. (1)

8.

___ Everything I believe to be true is worth fighting for, no matter how small. (1)

___ I fight for the things I believe in, but I know when to call a "cease-fire." (2)

___ I know which battles are worth fighting and which are better left alone. (3)

9.

___ I expect that things will always work out the way I planned. (1)

___ I believe that things will usually work out the way I planned. (2)

___ I understand that things don't always work out the way I planned. (3)

10.

___ I believe knowing what's important is the key to happiness. (3)

___ Fighting for the things I believe in is essential to my happiness. (2)

___ My prescription for happiness is to win every argument. (1)

Score: 21–30, you choose your battles wisely; 11–20, you still need some practice in deciding what's important to you; 1–10, you may be writing yourself a prescription for unhappiness and frustration. Choose your battles wisely and there may come a day when you won't need to do battle at all!

31.

Become Aware of Your Moods, and Don't Allow Yourself to Be Fooled by the Low Ones

Your moods can be extremely deceptive. When you're in a good mood, life looks great. When you're in a bad mood, life looks unbearable. Here's the catch: Moods are always on the run. The truth is, life is almost *never* as bad as it seems when you're in a low mood.

Are you sometimes fooled by your moods? If so, then think about the following.

1. Do you consider yourself moody?

2. How aware are you of your moods?

3. Which of the following describes you when you're in a bad mood (check all that apply).

____ irritable

____ impatient

____ sarcastic

____ critical

____ cynical

____ indecisive

____ rushing to judgment

4. Are others aware of your bad mood before you are?

5. When you're in a bad mood, how do you express it?

6. When you're in a bad mood, how long do you stay that way?

7. List what triggers your bad moods.

8. List the things that make you happy, and that can turn your mood around.

9. Do you sometimes find yourself in a bad mood for no reason?

10. Do you sometimes make important decisions while you're in a bad mood?

11. Did you ever do or say something while you were in a bad mood that you later regretted?

12. When I'm in a bad mood, here's how the world seems to me (check all that apply):

    ____ work is more difficult

    ____ everything becomes a bigger challenge

    ____ slight criticisms become huge personal insults

    ____ molehills become mountains

    ____ people's shortcomings become intentional acts of meanness

    ____ impersonal realities (like bus delays or telephone busy signals) are taken personally

    ____ home or working conditions become impossible to deal with

    ____ people are unreasonable

13. Have you ever postponed a meeting or deferred making a decision until you were in a better mood? Would you ever consider doing so? Why or why not?

32.

Life Is a Test. It Is Only a Test.

When you look at life and its many challenges as a test, you begin to see each issue you face as an opportunity to grow. If, on the other hand, you see each new issue you face as a battle that must be won, you're probably in for a very rocky journey.

Do you see life as a test? Below is a list of situations. For each one, write a short description of how you handled a recent occurrence. If you faced it as a battle, how could you have seen it instead as an opportunity to grow?

1. A disagreement with a family member over money

2. A disagreement with a family member over how to spend your time

3. Something you did that bothered a close friend

4. Something a close friend did that bothered you

5. A child's demand

6. A disagreement with a religious or other spiritual leader

7. A disagreement with a business owner or clerk

8. Trying to get service in a restaurant

9. Feeling stressed out in the face of too large a "to do" list

10. Your inability to successfully complete a home repair job

11. Keeping your weight where you want it

12. Staying on your exercise program

13. Keeping your room or house as neat as you would like

14. Being reprimanded at work

15. Having to reprimand someone at work

16. What you thought of as an unfair task at work

17. Being resentful over having to clean up after someone at work or at home

18. Getting a good parking space

19. Getting someone who's always late to be somewhere on time

20. Finding time to relax

33.

Praise and Blame Are All the Same

Everyone has their own set of ideas with which to evaluate life, and our ideas don't always match those of other people. For some reason, however, most of us get angry, hurt, or otherwise frustrated when people reject our ideas, tell us no, or give us some other form of disapproval. The sooner we accept the idea of not being able to win the approval of everyone we meet, the easier our lives will become.

Are praise and blame all the same to you? Complete this inventory to find out. Read all three statements and decide which one best describes your situation. Then write the point value in the space beside that statement.

1. When I wear something new for the first time
___ I always seek approval. (1)
___ I never seek approval. (3)
___ I might seek approval. (2)

2. Someone tells me I don't look well, even though I feel fine. I
___ worry about my appearance and ask others what they think. (2)
___ get depressed and hide myself away. (1)
___ try not to worry about it; maybe that person is having a bad day. (3)

3. If my spouse isn't happy with a new recipe,
___ I sometimes get upset. (2)
___ I never get upset. (3)
___ I always get upset. (1)

4. My idea for a community fund-raiser is turned down. I
___ gracefully accept that another idea is better than mine. (3)
___ feel that all my ideas are worthless and never suggest anything again. (1)
___ feel slightly hurt but understand their decision. (2)

5. If my local paper printed a letter I wrote to the editor, I would
___ maybe show my friends, neighbors, and coworkers. (2)

___ definitely show the article to everyone I know. (1)

___ show the article to a few select friends. (3)

6. My chili is a big success at the yearly Super Bowl party. I

___ modestly thank those who compliment me on it. (3)

___ tell everyone who doesn't already know that I made the chili. (1)

___ tell those who compliment me how difficult the chili is to make. (2)

7. My mother thanks me for flowers I sent her on Mother's Day. I

___ ask if my brother remembered to send flowers. (2)

___ praise myself for my wonderful selection. (1)

___ tell her that I'm glad she likes them. (3)

8. My spouse is upset that I forgot our anniversary. I

___ feel terrible and take my spouse to a favorite restaurant the following week. (3)

___ feel terrible and take my spouse to the most expensive restaurant in town. (1)

___ feel terrible and make a special dinner for my spouse right then and there. (2)

9. A neighbor thanks me for house-sitting on the spur of the moment. I

___ tell others about the nice thing I did for my neighbor. (1)

___ tell my neighbor in detail how I watered the flowers and fed the cat. (2)

___ exclaim that that's what neighbors are for. (3)

10. A coworker tells me to mind my own business after I try to help with an office problem. I

___ might be hurt by my coworker's harsh words. (2)

___ would not be hurt, but chalk it up to my coworker's stress. (3)

___ would definitely be hurt and never offer advice again. (1)

Score: 21–30, you don't need the constant approval of others to feel good about yourself; 11–20, certain kinds of disapproval bother you, while others do not; 1–10, say this phrase over and over to yourself, like a mantra: praise and blame are all the same. You'll soon realize that they are.

34.

Practice Random Acts of Kindness

Practicing random acts of kindness is an effective way to get in touch with the joy of giving without expecting anything in return. Each act of kindness rewards you with positive feelings and reminds you of the important aspects of life—service, kindness, and love.

1. Make a list of five random acts of kindness you can practice in each of the following situations. After each act, write down how long it would take and how much it would cost you to perform this act of kindness

AT YOUR JOB	TIME SPENT	COST
1. _____	_____	_____
2. _____	_____	_____
3. _____	_____	_____
4. _____	_____	_____
5. _____	_____	_____

AT THE MALL		
1. _____	_____	_____
2. _____	_____	_____
3. _____	_____	_____
4. _____	_____	_____
5. _____	_____	_____

BEHIND THE WHEEL		
1. _____	_____	_____
2. _____	_____	_____

3. _____ _____ _____

4. _____ _____ _____

5. _____ _____ _____

ON THE PHONE

1. _____ _____ _____

2. _____ _____ _____

3. _____ _____ _____

4. _____ _____ _____

5. _____ _____ _____

ON THE STREET

1. _____ _____ _____

2. _____ _____ _____

3. _____ _____ _____

4. _____ _____ _____

5. _____ _____ _____

2. Make a list of all the reasons you can think of *not* to perform random acts of kindness.

3. Look at the list you just made. Circle all the reasons that outweigh the benefits of performing random acts of kindness.

35.

Look Beyond Behavior

When we look beyond behavior, we have the perspective to give others the benefit of the doubt. It's easier than you might think. Try it today, and you'll see some nice results.

Are you able to look beyond an instance of someone behaving negatively without thinking that the person has it in for you? For each behavior below, fill in how you (a) could see it in the worst light, and (b) could look beyond the behavior to see what's really going on.

1. You and your best friend always kid around about his baldness. Today he snaps at you.
   a) _____
   b) _____

2. Your assistant always gets your morning coffee. Today he says, "Get your own coffee."
   a) _____
   b) _____

3. Your loved one always remembers the anniversary of the day you two met—until today.
   a) _____
   b) _____

4. After a business lunch, you discreetly mention a food stain on the jacket of a colleague. He or she snaps, "Why don't you broadcast it to everyone?"
   a) _____
   b) _____

5. You have just delivered a bag of groceries to your housebound neighbor. The store was out of one brand of an item so you substituted another. Before you can explain, your neighbor says, "You idiot! You got the wrong brand!"
   a) _____
   b) _____

6. You're sitting at your desk trying to figure out a work-related problem when your boss comes by. "I don't pay you to daydream," she says, and leaves before you can say a word.

a) _____

b) _____

7. You come home after a hard day at the office, expecting your work-at-home mate to have dinner ready. He says, "You think I sit around here all day enjoying myself?"

a) _____

b) _____

8. You come out of the house one morning and discover that your neighbor has dumped a whole pile of leaves on your side of the common lawn.

a) _____

b) _____

9. It's time for your favorite TV show, and your roommate is carrying on a loud phone conversation nearby. When asked to move it to a different room, she shouts, "I was here first!"

a) _____

b) _____

10. While your child is taking a bath, you lay out clothes for her to wear to school the next day. When she sees them, she comes running in to you, screaming, "How could you do this? You want me to look like a geek!"

a) _____

b) _____

11. You call your mother every Thursday night. Tonight you come home late from a business dinner and it's almost ten when you call. She snaps, "Too busy for your mother?"

a) _____

b) _____

36.

See the Innocence

When someone is acting in a way that we don't like, the best strategy for dealing with that person is to distance ourselves from the behavior and see the innocence in where the behavior is coming from. This shift in thinking can often put us into a state of compassion.

Are you able to see the innocence? The true/false exercise below will help you isolate your problem areas in seeing the innocence in others.

When people yell at me, I take it personally.	T	F
First impressions are usually correct.	T	F
Sometimes I'll yell at a person even when I know it's not his or her fault.	T	F
Often, I misjudge people based on inadequate information about them.	T	F
Some people use arrogance to mask their insecurities.	T	F
How I act depends on whom I'm with.	T	F
If a person unintentionally hurts my feelings, I'll tell him or her.	T	F
If someone is acting angry, I respond in anger.	T	F
If someone acts insensitively, I shrug it off.	T	F
If someone is being cruel, I confront him or her about it.	T	F
It's okay for people to show anger sometimes.	T	F
Some people are, by nature, irritating to everyone around them.	T	F
If someone is behaving irrationally, there's probably a rational explanation that I don't know about.	T	F
It's easy to make snap decisions about why people behave the way they do.	T	F

1. List the types of people that make you angry or irritated.

2. List ways you might try to see the innocence of these people and avoid becoming angry or irritated with them.

3. List the situations that make you angry or irritated.

4. In the cases above, if you take out your frustrations on the people around you, list ways to adjust your attitude to see the innocence of each situation.

37.

Choose Being Kind over Being Right

If you pay attention to the way you feel after you put someone down, you'll notice that you feel worse than before the put-down. It's impossible to feel better at the expense of someone else. Luckily, the opposite is true—when your goal is to build someone up, you, too, reap the rewards of their positive feelings.

Would you rather be kind than be right? Complete this inventory to find out. Read all three statements and decide which one best describes your situation. Then write the point value in the space beside that statement.

1. I attend a community theater production of a show I saw on Broadway. I
____ congratulate the cast for a wonderful performance. (3)
____ keep my mouth shut; the show is not as good as the Broadway version. (2)
____ point out to others how the Broadway show was better. (1)

2. The community bake sale fund-raiser was a huge success, and my contributions sold the most. I
____ figure out what percentage of the funds my foods brought in. (2)
____ celebrate happily over the success of the fund-raiser. (3)
____ make sure everyone knows that my foods brought in the most money. (1)

3. A group project at work is hailed as creative. It was my original idea. I
____ make sure the company newsletter prints whose idea it was. (1)
____ make sure the colleagues in my group remember it was my idea. (2)
____ accept the praise along with my coworkers. (3)

4. My game-ending catch wins my team the county softball championship. I
____ modestly thank reporters for their praise. (2)
____ tell reporters it was a team effort. (3)
____ remind reporters that if it wasn't for me, the team would not have won. (1)

5. On my advice, a friend loses a lot of weight. I
____ enjoy the compliments my friend now receives. (3)

___ tell others that my friend's change is due to my advice. (2)

___ point out that my friend looks great but now needs a new wardrobe. (1)

6. A coworker is excited about a new job opportunity. I

___ point out that more work might be involved. (1)

___ am interested and ask questions about it. (3)

___ encourage my coworker, then change the subject. (2)

7. I made the costumes for a holiday pageant at school, but the teacher gets the praise. I

___ agree with everyone that the show is a success. (3)

___ agree that the show is a success and ask what they thought about the costumes. (2)

___ agree that the show is a success and remind them that I made the costumes. (1)

8. A friend has borrowed an item of clothing and receives many compliments on it. I

___ might point out that the article of clothing is mine. (2)

___ would definitely point out that the article of clothing is mine. (1)

___ would never point out that the article of clothing is mine. (3)

9. A friend is happy about buying an expensive collectible that I think is silly. I

___ tell my friend exactly what I think. (1)

___ share in my friend's happiness. (3)

___ tell my friend it's nice, but isn't it a little expensive? (2)

10. I've had a bad meal at a trendy new restaurant that my friends are excited to go to. I

___ decide not to go but don't tell them why. (2)

___ relate my horrible experience so they'll change their minds. (1)

___ decide to go and try the restaurant again. (3)

Score: 21–30, you refrain from being right at the expense of others' feelings; 11–20, you still need to practice being a bit more kind; 1–10, you tend to point out to others your own accomplishments or the flaws in something. Instead, try to enjoy the moments of joy with those around you.

38.

Tell Three People (Today) How Much You Love Them

What are you waiting for? Now is the time to let people know how much you care. If you're too shy to make a phone call, write a heartfelt letter instead. As you get used to letting people know how much you love them, it will become a regular part of your life.

Start right now. Make a list of three people you love. In the spaces below, write the name of each one. Then imagine the dialogue that might take place between you and each of these people as they receive your message of love.

Recipient of love no. 1 _____

Recipient of love no. 2 _____

Recipient of love no. 3 _____

1. Think about how you may have felt *just before* you told these people how much you loved them. You might have been nervous, scared, excited, or all of the above. List several words or phrases to describe the way you felt.

2. Think about how each recipient of love may have felt upon hearing your message. They might have been surprised, gratified, overwhelmed, or all of the above. List several words or phrases to describe their reactions.

3. Now think about how you feel *right now* for having let people know how much you love them. List several words or phrases to describe the way you feel.

4. Would you tell people how much you love them again? Why or why not?

39.

Practice Humility

It takes a lot of energy to be continually pointing out your accomplishments, bragging, or trying to convince others of your worth as a human being. The more you try to prove yourself, the more others will try to avoid you.

People are drawn to those with a quiet, inner confidence: people who don't need to *make* themselves look good, people who practice humility.

Do *you* practice humility? Let this questionnaire help you find out. For **no**, score 0; for **sometimes**, score 1; for **often**, score 2.

1. Before I meet someone new, I think of how to impress that person. ____

2. I sneak my college grade point average into casual conversation. ____

3. I like to tell people about the bonus I expect to get at the end of the year. ____

4. I believe that where I live is an indication of how good a person I am. ____

5. If a friend tells me something good about his or her child, I can't resist finding a way to brag about a child of mine (or another child I'm close to). ____

6. If someone at work tells me of something bad that has happened to him or her, I think it's important to tell that person about something bad that's happened to me. ____

7. I think I'm smarter than most of the people I know. ____

8. I think I'm harder to fool than most of the people I know. ____

9. I like to tell people about all the bargains I get when I go shopping. ____

10. While with friends in a restaurant they love, I rave about the food elsewhere. ____

11. While eating dinner at a friend's house, I like to describe in detail the delicious food I have prepared on previous occasions. ____

12. I tell people I had the best childhood I can imagine. ____

13. I tell people I had the worst childhood I can imagine. ____

14. I know the best places to go on vacation. ____

15. I tell people that my house is the best-maintained house on the block. ____

16. I tell people not to buy a car before consulting with me. ____

17. I hate when someone else gets credit for something I've done, and I make sure to point it out. ____

18. I make sure to order the wine in a restaurant. ____

19. I think I'm the best athlete. ____

20. I like to tell people stories about my glory days. ____

21. I tell people my spouse (partner, person I'm dating) is the best cook. ____

22. I think I would be a great guest of honor at a testimonial dinner. ____

23. I find it hard to express admiration for people. ____

24. I find it hard to express admiration for people without thinking of something for which I should be admired. ____

25. I don't like to see others being praised. ____

26. I want people to think I'm the most valuable employee where I work. ____

27. I enjoy pointing out the failures of others. ____

28. I enjoy watching others fail, then coming in and doing the thing the right way. ____

29. I question the rules. ____

30. I find it hard to believe that people don't want to do things my way. ____

31. I believe I have a superior understanding of the world. ____

32. I believe I have special gifts and talents. ____

Score: Add up the total of your responses. The lower you score, the more humble you are. If you score 10 or less, other people may find you just too good to be true. If you score much above 32, eat humble pie soon!

40.

When in Doubt about Whose Turn It Is to Take Out the Trash, Go Ahead and Take It Out

It's difficult to become a contented person if you're keeping score of all you do. Keeping track only clutters your mind with who's doing what, who's doing more, and so forth. If you want to know the truth, this is the epitome of "small stuff." It will bring far more joy to your life to know that you have done your part.

Do you keep score? Put a check mark in the box beside each area where the question "Whose turn is it?" is cluttering your mind.

___ Taking out the trash

___ Vacuuming

___ Cleaning the bathroom

___ Doing the dishes

___ Doing the laundry

___ Turning out the lights

___ Watering the plants

___ Cleaning the closets

___ Cleaning the basement or attic

___ Mowing the lawn

___ Raking leaves

___ Shoveling snow

___ Taking the dog out

___ Emptying the litter box

___ Attending to the crying baby

___ Thinking of what to have for dinner

___ Preparing dinner

___ Calling for dinner delivery

___ Going for takeout

___ Making dinner reservations

___ Paying for dinner

___ Remembering to tape a TV show

___ Resetting the clocks for daylight/standard time

___ Replacing the batteries in the smoke detector

___ Picking up the dry cleaning

___ Taking the car in for servicing

___ Driving in the car pool

___ Phoning or E-mailing

___ Remembering Grandma's birthday

___ Buying the card or gift

___ Buying the Halloween candy

___ Giving candy out to the trick-or-treaters

___ Putting up the Christmas decorations

___ Tipping the doorman at Christmas

___ Sending out the Christmas cards

___ Making vacation reservations

___ Stopping the newspaper delivery before going on vacation

___ Calling friends to make social arrangements

___ Saying "I love you"

41.

Avoid Weatherproofing

Just as we can weatherproof a home for the winter by looking for cracks, leaks, and imperfections, we can also weatherproof our relationships, even our lives, by doing the very same thing. Are you on the lookout for what needs to be fixed or repaired? Do you find all the cracks and flaws in life? Not only does this alienate you from other people, it makes you feel bad, too. It encourages you to think about what's *wrong* with everything and everyone.

Do you weatherproof your relationships, certain aspects of your life, or both? Complete this inventory to find out. Read all three statements and decide which one best describes your situation. Then write the point value in the space beside that statement.

1. My spouse's morning cheerfulness is a source of irritation for me. I
___ point out each morning that no one should be happy so early. (1)
___ point out occasionally that I find my spouse's early-morning mood irritating. (2)
___ try to see my spouse's attitude as a positive way to greet the day. (3)

2. I'm always picking up my neighbors' trash cans after they blow into the street. I
___ make sure each time that my neighbors know what a bother this is. (1)
___ return the trash cans to their proper place and don't think twice about it. (3)
___ sometimes make fun of my neighbors' apparent aversion to replacing the cans. (2)

3. I am seeing someone new, but he or she likes music I really don't enjoy. I
___ listen to the music to gain an appreciation for it. (3)
___ try to make that person change his or her taste in music. (1)
___ sometimes complain about his or her choice in music. (2)

4. While watching a sporting event, I realize that my new coworker is a poor loser. I
___ make a few jokes about my coworker's passionate attitude. (2)
___ accept my coworker for whom she or he is. (3)
___ tell everyone the next day what a poor loser our new coworker is. (1)

5. My parents have started telling me all about their friends' ailments. I
___ listen attentively and with compassion. (3)
___ tell them I don't care or have time to listen about their friends. (1)
___ listen the first few times, then try to limit this topic of conversation. (2)

6. Someone I recently met has the irritating habit of being an expert on *everything*. I would
___ definitely point out that I find this habit irritating. (1)
___ let the person know that I know something about the subject, too. (2)
___ encourage the person to share, then add my own thoughts. (3)

7. As I get to know someone and pick up on an annoying habit of theirs, I
___ might point out the flaw—that's my duty as a friend, right? (2)
___ probably would not say anything—I'm not perfect, either. (3)
___ would say something right away—I can't be around someone who does that. (1)

8. My sibling has the annoying habit of putting his newborn baby on the phone. I
___ point out to my sibling how much this annoys me. (1)
___ understand my sibling's happiness and enjoy the moment. (3)
___ put up with this silliness occasionally. (2)

9. My best friend is dating someone new who does certain things that I find strange. I
___ keep my opinion to myself. (3)
___ tell my friend one time what I think. (2)
___ point out to my friend every time his or her date does those things. (1)

10. A colleague who frequently invites me to lunch is always late. I
___ point out on occasion how long I've been waiting. (2)
___ plan for my colleague to be late and do something in the meantime. (3)
___ make a big deal about it every time my colleague shows up. (1)

Score: 21–30, you accept people and things the way they are; 11–20, you still let some imperfections bother you. Try to be a bit more accepting; 1–10, you are still too judgmental. Work a bit harder to accept the people and things around you, without being so critical.

42.

Spend a Moment, Every Day, Thinking of Someone to Love

When you wake up tomorrow morning, ask yourself, "Who shall I send love to today?" Most likely, a picture of someone will pop into your mind—a family member, a friend, someone you work with, a neighbor. It really doesn't matter who it is; the idea is to gear your mind toward love.

Can you spend a moment each day thinking of someone to love? Try to think of a reason to thank each of the following people in your life, and write it in the blank.

MOTHER _____

FATHER _____

BROTHER _____

SISTER _____

GRANDMOTHER _____

GRANDFATHER _____

AUNT _____

UNCLE _____

COUSIN _____

CHILD _____

GRANDCHILD _____

SPOUSE _____

EX-SPOUSE _____

SOMEONE YOU'RE DATING _____

SOMEONE YOU USED TO DATE _____

RELIGIOUS LEADER _____

POLITICAL LEADER _____

NEIGHBOR _____

TEACHER _____

COACH _____

FRIEND _____

EMPLOYER _____

COLLEAGUE _____

ASSISTANT _____

FINANCIAL ADVISOR _____

DOCTOR _____

LAWYER _____

REALTOR _____

TRAVEL AGENT _____

HOTEL CLERK _____

WAITER _____

RECEPTIONIST _____

STORE CLERK _____

DELIVERY PERSON _____

POLICE OFFICER _____

REPAIR PERSON _____

ENTERTAINER (WHO YOU DON'T PERSONALLY KNOW) _____

PET _____

43.

Become an Anthropologist

Anthropology, defined as "being interested, without judgment, in the way other people choose to live and behave," is a strategy geared toward developing your compassion. It replaces judgments with lovingkindness, and can make you less frustrated by the actions of others.

Are you an anthropologist? The true/false exercise below will help you isolate your problem areas as you try to be less judgmental.

When I mingle at a party, I generally approach people who look and act like me.	T	F
Most of my friends have the same economic background as I do.	T	F
I don't think I would have much in common with someone with different religious beliefs.	T	F
Kids today frighten me.	T	F
I'm quick to pass judgment on people based on their clothes.	T	F
People with low-paying jobs are probably less intelligent.	T	F
People with physical disabilities make me nervous.	T	F
Quiet people are usually insecure.	T	F
People who drive sports cars are reckless.	T	F
Nobody would really choose to live in an apartment if they could afford a house.	T	F
Overweight people are unhappy with their lives.	T	F
People who skydive have a death wish.	T	F
When I meet people one of the first things I ask is what they do for a living.	T	F

1. Write down what the following say about you.

   Your neighborhood
   Your clothes

Your job

Your friends

Your hobbies

2. If someone were to see you for the first time, what would he or she be able to tell about you, before you even had a chance to speak?

3. List some qualities about yourself that someone wouldn't discover until they really got to know you.

44.

Understand Separate Realities

If you've traveled to foreign countries, you are aware of the vast differences among cultures. The idea of separate realities is that the differences among individuals are every bit as vast. Just as we wouldn't expect people of different cultures to see or do things as we would, the individual differences in our ways of seeing the world would prohibit this as well. By respecting the fact that we're all different, we will increase our love for others—and ourselves.

Do you understand the principle of separate realities? Read the statements below. Circle T (**true**) or F (**false**) according to whether or not each statement applies to you. Be sure to respond as you are right now, not as you'd like to be.

I have a hard time relating to people who keep a strict nine-to-five schedule
at work.   T   F

I can't understand why anyone would commute to a job for more than an
hour a day.   T   F

I can't imagine why anyone would prefer dining out to a having a meal
cooked at home.   T   F

I don't know why some people insist on trying to look younger than they are. T   F

I have a hard time understanding people who keep their feelings locked inside
them.   T   F

I can't relate to perfectionists. After all, we all make mistakes!   T   F

I don't understand why some people would choose *not* to have children.   T   F

I don't understand how some people can find exercising relaxing and
enjoyable.   T   F

I can't imagine how anyone can make vegetarianism a way of life.   T   F

I can't relate to people who work around the clock. They need to put more
fun in their lives.   T   F

I don't understand why so many people are afraid of computers and
technology.   T   F

1. Look over your responses. Each statement that you have marked *true* represents a perspective you find hard to understand. Try the following exercise:

   - Choose one statement you marked *true*.
   - Argue *for* that perspective in the space below.
     List at least three reasons why a person might have that point of view.
   - Now repeat this procedure for each statement you marked *true*.

2. Does this exercise give you a better understanding of the principle of separate realities?
   Why or why not?

45.

Develop Your Own Helping Rituals

It's helpful to do kind, peaceful things. One way to do this is by developing your own helping rituals. You might pick up litter, shovel snow from someone's driveway, or help an elderly person cross the street.

Do you have your own helping rituals? If not, think about the following.

1. Think about an area in your home. How might you make it a little better?

2. Think about someone in your family. How might you make his or her life a little better?

3. Think about an area in your neighborhood. How might you make it a little better?

4. Think about someone you know. How might you make his or her day a little better?

5. Think about five times when you could have offered kindness, but chose not to. For example, perhaps you saw your neighbor's newspaper lying outside in the rain. Or watched as a neighbor was unloading a heavy item. Or perhaps you saw litter along the street in front of your house. List five instances below.

a.

b.

c.

d.

e.

6. Now write what you could have done to help.

a.

b.

c.

d.

e.

7. Choose the ritual of kindness that you find comes most easily to you. Write it here. Try to make your helping ritual part of your routine!

46.

Every Day, Tell at Least One Person Something You Like, Admire, or Appreciate about Them

Many people spend their entire lifetimes wishing that other people would acknowledge them. Letting someone know how you feel about them is a gesture of lovingkindness. Try the following.

1. Make a list of people you like, admire, or appreciate.

2. Next to each name on your list, write down what you admire or appreciate most about them.

3. What scares you most about expressing your admiration?

4. What's the nicest compliment you've received?

5. How did you feel afterward?

6. What have you always wanted to hear someone say to you?

7. Have you ever said this to someone else? Why or why not?

8. Compliments don't always have to be about big issues; they just have to be sincere. If you're new at expressing your admiration, start off slow until your confidence builds. Rank each of the following items or characteristics from 1 to 18, according to how comfortable you'd be paying someone a compliment about it.

____ clothing

____ hair

____ car

____ house

____ smile

____ laugh

____ sense of humor

____ taste in art

____ diplomacy skills

____ eyes

____ outlook on life

____ attitude

___ job skills

___ tenacity

___ fragrance

___ devotion to duty

___ family

___ cooking

47.

Argue for Your Limitations, and They're Yours

Our minds are powerful tools. When we decide that something is beyond our reach, it's very difficult to pierce through this self-created hurdle. Don't argue for your own limitations! This negative habit can easily be replaced by something more positive.

Do you argue for your own limitations? Complete this inventory to find out. Statements are presented in sets of three. Each one has a point value. Read all three statements and decide which one best describes your situation. Then write the point value in the space beside that statement.

1. I am presented with a new project at work. I
—— look for reasons why I can't do it. (1)
—— look forward to the challenge. (3)
—— take on the project but tell others why I might have problems with it. (2)

2. My friends want me to join a gym with them. I
—— declare that I've always been a klutz and shouldn't go. (1)
—— am not too sure of the idea, but give it a try with an open mind. (3)
—— tell my friends that I am very busy and can probably go only once. (2)

3. My coworkers decide to start a softball team. I
—— say I'll try it, but I'll probably make the team lose. (1)
—— say I'll try it, but that I was awful at sports in school. (2)
—— say I'll try it and thank them for asking me to join. (3)

4. I'm about to drive to a friend's new house for a dinner party. I tell my friend
—— not to hold dinner if I'm late—you never know how traffic will be. (2)
—— to forgive me if I'm late—I have an awful sense of direction. (1)
—— that I look forward to seeing the new house. (3)

5. My neighbors think it would be fun to go holiday caroling. I
—— tell them I'll join them and bring the hot chocolate. (3)

___ tell them I'll join them, but that I can't sing. (1)

___ tell them I'll join them, but I hope none of my coworkers see me. (2)

6. My friends convince me to buy a raffle ticket for charity. I

___ mention that I don't know why I bother—I never win anything. (1)

___ think it's a great idea—someone has to win. (3)

___ shove the ticket in my pocket—raffles are stupid. (2)

7. My spouse plans an exciting weekend getaway to Las Vegas. I point out that

___ I never have any luck, so why bother? (1)

___ we have too many things going on right now to enjoy ourselves. (2)

___ I've always wanted to go, and it will be a fun time. (3)

8. I wish to discuss a problem with my spouse. I think that

___ we can discuss the problem and reach an equitable agreement. (3)

___ we'll only end up arguing—no one understands me. (1)

___ I should just not bring up the problem—why look for trouble? (2)

9. I've finally decided that I seriously want to start a diet. I

___ know that this time I will be successful. (3)

___ am honest with myself that I have no willpower. (2)

___ remember when I've failed at diets in the past. (1)

10. My spouse thinks it would be good for us to take a ballroom dancing class. I

___ agree to go, but know that you can't teach an old dog new tricks. (1)

___ agree to go, only because my spouse wants me to. (2)

___ agree to go and have a good time. (3)

Score: 21–30, you try not to see the brick walls in things, only the endless possibilities; 11–20, you can see what you are aiming for, but you tend to see obstacles, too; 1–10, you probably feel weighed down by all the negatives. Practice telling yourself, "I can," rather than, "I can't."

48.
Remember That Everything Has God's Fingerprints on It

It's easy to see the holiness of a beautiful landscape or a newborn child. But can we learn to find the holiness in difficult life lessons or a family tragedy? When we fill our life with the desire to see the holiness in everyday things, a feeling of peace emerges. We remember that everything has God's fingerprints on it.

Are you looking with a broad perspective to find the holiness in everyday things? Complete this inventory to find out. Read all three statements and decide which one best describes your situation. Then write the point value in the space beside that statement.

1. If I lost my job, I would
—— be sad, but would look for a new one. (2)
—— think that something better was waiting for me. (3)
—— complain and collect unemployment. (1)

2. I make the error that causes my office softball team to lose the corporate
   challenge. I
—— most likely lament the fact that bad things always happen to me. (1)
—— possibly lament the fact that bad things always happen to me. (2)
—— do not lament—the other team needs the victory more to bolster morale. (3)

3. My pet is killed when it is hit by a car. I
—— go to the pound to give another animal a good home. (3)
—— declare that I will never have a pet again, it's too painful. (1)
—— give myself some time to recover from the loss of my pet. (2)

4. I receive a speeding ticket when I am only going with the flow of traffic. I feel that
—— I am unjustly singled out for the violation, but accept it. (2)
—— I should fight the ticket in court. (1)
—— perhaps I was going too fast and the officer saved me from an accident. (3)

5. If I were stuck in an elevator, I would
___ try to relax and use the moment for some quiet, personal time. (3)
___ panic and make everyone around me panic. (1)
___ wonder why this happened. (2)

6. If I was turned down for a promotion at work, I would
___ probably ask my boss why. (2)
___ rationalize that the job would have been more than I could handle. (3)
___ complain to my coworkers about how insulted I am. (1)

7. I put money in a candy vending machine, but nothing comes out. I
___ realize that I really don't need to eat candy anyway. (3)
___ wonder why bad things happen to me. (1)
___ try to find a candy machine that works. (2)

8. If I came down with a terrible case of the flu, I would
___ most likely become stressed out over all the work I was missing. (1)
___ worry about work only occasionally. (2)
___ not worry about work much, but take the opportunity to start that book I'd been
trying to read. (3)

9. Without trying it on, I buy a piece of clothing on sale that is nonreturnable, only to
realize it doesn't fit. I
___ donate it to a homeless shelter; someone can use it. (3)
___ wonder why things like this always happen and stuff the clothing in a drawer. (1)
___ get a good laugh over my mistake with my friends. (2)

10. Longtime neighbors are moving away due to a job transfer. I
___ might resent whoever moves into their house. (2)
___ will definitely not be friends with my new neighbors. (1)
___ will definitely welcome my new neighbors. (3)

Score: 21–30, you can see the silver lining in even the darkest cloud; 11–20, try to
realize that even bad situations have a reason for happening; 1–10, you need to reevaluate
ate situations to see a "higher" purpose, no matter how bleak those situations may
appear to be.

49.

Resist the Urge to Criticize

When we criticize another person, it says nothing about that person. Instead, it says something about our own need to be critical. Criticism is nothing more than a bad habit. Think about how you feel immediately after you criticize someone. Likely, you feel deflated and ashamed, almost as if *you're the* one who has been attacked.

Can you resist the urge to criticize? The exercises below are designed to give you practice in turning the act of being critical into something more productive.

1. Your child comes home with one bad grade on the report card. Your critical response might be,

   But instead you say,

2. You and your neighbor arrange to take turns bringing trash to a recycling center. This morning, your neighbor forgot whose turn it was—and there sits the garbage! Your critical response might be,

   But instead you say,

3. You dislike a particular sweater that your spouse likes immensely. It gets worn a lot! Your critical response might be,

But instead you say,

4. Your teenager is blaring music from the bedroom—and it's not the kind you really want to hear. Your critical response might be,

But instead you say,

5. Conversation at an office party turns to bad-mouthing the boss. Your impulse to criticize was great last year. In fact, you said,

But this year you say,

6. Your new office at work is not what you'd wish for. Still it comes with a promotion, more money—and a new title! Your critical response might be,

But instead you say,

7. Your assistant has a habit of humming that you simply cannot stand. Your critical response might be,

But instead you say,

8. Your children think a new sitcom is not only funny, but hilarious. You think it's dopey, but you allow them one show a week that's completely their choice. Your critical response might be,

But instead you say,

9. Your sister just restyled her hair—a new cut, a new color! You find it unflattering. Your critical response might be,

But instead you say,

10. Two people at work have just told you how much they loved a new "trash novel" by a particular author. You *hate* trash novels and don't much like the author. Your critical response might be,

But instead you say,

50.

Write Down Your Five Most Stubborn Positions and See If You Can Soften Them

It doesn't make you weak to soften your positions. In fact, it makes you stronger. Becoming wiser and gentler might just improve your relationships in life.

Write down your five most stubborn positions below. Make a list of the reasons why you have been reluctant to give each one up. Then make a list of some positive things that might happen if you soften each position.

1. Stubborn position 1:

Why I haven't been able to give it up:

The benefits of softening (or giving up) this position are:

2. Stubborn position 2:

Why I haven't been able to give it up:

The benefits of softening (or giving up) this position are:

3. Stubborn position 3:

Why I haven't been able to give it up:

The benefits of softening (or giving up) this position are:

4. Stubborn position 4:

Why I haven't been able to give it up:

The benefits of softening (or giving up) this position are:

5. Stubborn position 5:

Why I haven't been able to give it up:

The benefits of softening (or giving up) this position are:

51.

Just for Fun, Agree with Criticism Directed Toward You (Then Watch It Go Away)

So often we treat criticism like an emergency and defend ourselves as if we were in a battle. All this reaction takes an enormous amount of mental energy. A useful exercise is to agree with criticism directed toward you. Not only does this defuse the situation, but it can offer you a chance to learn something about yourself by seeing a grain of truth in another point of view.

Are you immobilized by the slightest criticism? The exercises below are designed to give you practice in turning defensive responses into learning situations.

1. Your best friend tells you that your friendship is becoming a little too one-sided. Your first response is to defend yourself by saying,

   But instead you agree with your friend and say,

2. Your boss says you don't speak up at meetings. Your first response is to defend yourself by saying,

   But instead you agree with your boss and say,

3. Your spouse says you're too "closed-up" lately. You keep all your feelings locked inside. Your first response is to defend yourself by saying,

But instead you agree with your spouse and say,

4. Your assistant tells you that you don't take the time to teach her what she needs to know. Your first response is to defend yourself by saying,

But instead you agree with your assistant and say,

5. Your children say you spend too much time at work and not enough time with them. Your first response is to defend yourself by saying,

But instead you agree with your children and say,

6. Your colleagues tell you that you tend to hog the spotlight. Your first reaction is to defend yourself by saying,

But instead you agree with your colleagues and say,

7. Your mother says you don't call her often enough. Your first reaction is to defend yourself by saying,

But instead you agree with your mother and say,

8. Your doctor says you don't get enough exercise. Your first reaction is to defend yourself by saying,

But instead you agree with your doctor and say,

9. Everyone tells you to "lighten up" lately. Your first reaction is to defend yourself by saying,

But instead you agree with everyone and say,

10. The bathroom scale tells you that you're gaining too much weight. Your first reaction is to defend yourself and say,

But instead you heed the warning of your bathroom scale and say,

52.

Search for the Grain of Truth in Others' Opinions

Almost everyone feels that their opinions are good ones or they wouldn't be sharing them with you. Remember that almost every opinion has some merit, especially if we are looking for merit, rather than looking for errors.

Can you find the grain of truth in other opinions? Try to think of an opinion recently expressed by each of the following people in your life—be sure it's one you've disagreed with! Write it on the first blank line. Now try to find the grain of truth in each of those positions. Write it down on the second line.

MOTHER'S OPINION _____

THE TRUTH OF IT IS _____

FATHER'S OPINION _____

THE TRUTH OF IT IS _____

BROTHER'S OPINION _____

THE TRUTH OF IT IS _____

SISTER'S OPINION _____

THE TRUTH OF IT IS _____

CHILD'S OPINION _____

THE TRUTH OF IT IS _____

SPOUSE'S OPINION _____

THE TRUTH OF IT IS _____

EX-SPOUSE'S OPINION _____

THE TRUTH OF IT IS _____

A DATE'S OPINION _____

THE TRUTH OF IT IS _____

A RELIGIOUS LEADER'S OPINION _____

THE TRUTH OF IT IS _____

A NEIGHBOR'S OPINION _____

THE TRUTH OF IT IS _____

A FRIEND'S OPINION _____

THE TRUTH OF IT IS _____

YOUR BOSS'S OPINION _____

THE TRUTH OF IT IS _____

A COLLEAGUE'S OPINION _____

THE TRUTH OF IT IS _____

A CLIENT'S OPINION _____

THE TRUTH OF IT IS _____

YOUR ASSISTANT'S OPINION _____

THE TRUTH OF IT IS _____

A MENTOR'S OPINION _____

THE TRUTH OF IT IS _____

YOUR DOCTOR'S OPINION _____

THE TRUTH OF IT IS _____

YOUR LAWYER'S OPINION _____

THE TRUTH OF IT IS _____

Score: Cross out any people who are not in your life. For each person in whose opinion you are able to find a grain of truth, score 1. Then divide your score by the total number of people left to get a percentage. If you score below 50%, you're looking for the errors rather than the merit in other opinions; 50%–75%, you sometimes look for the merit in other opinions; 75%–90%, you keep an open mind; above 90%, you clearly intend to find the grain of truth in other opinions.

53.

See the Glass as Already Broken (and Everything Else, Too)

Everything has a beginning and everything has an end. A glass is created and will eventually break. When you expect something to break, you are not surprised or disappointed when it does. You've made peace with the way things are.

Can *you* make peace with the way things are? If not, try the following.

1. Name something that became very important to you that was lost.

2. What was your initial response to the loss?

3. How did you overcome the feeling of loss?

4. In one or two sentences, write what you learned from the experience.

5. List the five most important things in your life right now. Include objects, people, your job, etc.

   a.

   b.

   c.

   d.

   e.

6. Next to each item, write why it is important to you.

7. What was your life like before these items became a part of it? (Each letter corresponds to one of the items on your list.)

   a.

   b.

   c.

   d.

   e.

8. Imagine each of these items disappearing from your life tomorrow. Would your life go back to the way it was before they became part of it? In what ways did they forever change your life? (Each letter corresponds to one of the items on your list.)

a.

b.

c.

d.

e.

9. "When I've lost something important to me, here's what I should do." Circle the responses below that will help you accept that the glass is broken.

Dwell on the loss	Deny my feelings
Cherish the good times I had	Learn to let go
Get angry	Accept reality
Feel sad	Rush to find a replacement
Find some distraction	Hide my pain
Beat myself up	Be forgiving
Realize that I can't change the situation	Assign blame

10. Did some of the choices seem ambiguous? List them and write down why you're not certain they'd be helpful reactions.

54.

Understand the Statement, "Wherever You Go, There You Are"

We tend to believe that if we were somewhere else—on vacation, with another partner, in a different career—somehow we would be happier and more content. We wouldn't! If you get annoyed and bothered easily, if you feel angry and frustrated, or if you wish things were different, these identical tendencies will follow you wherever you go. On the other hand, if you are generally a happy person, then you can move from place to place, from person to person, with very little negative impact.

Do you understand that "wherever you go, there you are"? If not, write the answers to the following.

1. List the major problems in your life right now.

2. In the above list, circle those problems that are long-term or recurring.
3. If you could make one major change in your life tomorrow (new job, new location, new relationship, etc.), what change would you make?

4. List five situations or problems that this change would solve.

   a.

   b.

   c.

   d.

   e.

5. On the list above, circle those items that you can change without moving or starting from scratch.

6. List five benefits you would gain by making a major change in your life.

   a.

   b.

   c.

   d.

   e.

7. On the list above, circle those items that you can achieve in your current situation.

8. List five negative things that will accompany you regardless of what you do to change your life. These can be physical things or attitudes.

   a.

   b.

   c.

   d.

   e.

9. On the list above, circle those items you've genuinely tried to change.

10. Take a good look at your current situation. List those things or situations that you didn't like at one time, but that no longer bother you.

11. What did you do to feel better about the situations you listed above? Try incorporating those strategies for each item on your list above.

55.

Breathe Before You Speak

Listening is one of the most treasured gifts you can offer. And it's a gift you can give through a simple strategy. It involves nothing more than pausing—breathing—after the person to whom you are speaking is finished. The almost immediate results include increased patience, added perspective, and the gratitude of others!

Observe yourself in conversations. Do you simply wait for *your* chance to speak? Or do you *really* listen to others? Take this questionnaire to find out. You may want to recall your answers *before* you get the urge to jump in and speak before breathing. For each answer, score 0 for **never**, 5 for **sometimes**, and 10 for **most of the time**.

1. Are you uncomfortable with pauses in conversations?   ___

2. Are you impatient with people who are slow to get to the point?   ___

3. Do you listen with half a brain while the other half plans what you're going to say?   ___

4. Do you anxiously wait for an opening—any opening—to express your point of view?   ___

5. Do you interrupt others or finish their sentences?   ___

6. Do you say "Yeah, yeah" or "I know" very rapidly to urge others to hurry up so you can have your turn?   ___

7. Do you criticize points of view or form opinions before others have finished speaking?   ___

8. Do you ever get the sense that you annoy, bother, or irritate your fellow communicators?   ___

9. When people pause to contemplate their answers, do you perceive great time gaps in the conversation?   ___

10. When people pause to take a breath before speaking, do you perceive an uncomfortable time gap in the conversation?   ___

Score: Less than 30, you prefer unhurried discourse; 30–60, you're short on patience and probably short on perspective about what's being said; 60–90, you may find people avoiding you in conversation; over 90, it's a wonder you have anyone to talk to!

Look over your responses. Circle the ones that relate to something you'd like to change. Write a few lines below about the changes you'd like to make for each one.

56.

Be Grateful When You're Feeling Good and Graceful When You're Feeling Bad

The happiest person on earth isn't always happy. Yet, peaceful, relaxed people, when they are feeling good, are very grateful. They understand that feelings come and go. There will come a time when they won't be feeling so good. To happy people, it's the way of things. So, when they are feeling low, they relate to that feeling with the same openness and wisdom, knowing this, too, shall pass.

What do *you* do when you are feeling low? If your answer to a question is **never**, circle 0; for **sometimes**, circle 1; for **often**, circle 2; for **always**, circle 3.

1. I tend to blame myself.	0	1	2	3
2. I tend to blame other people.	0	1	2	3
3. I take a personal inventory.	0	1	2	3
4. I complain to a loved one.	0	1	2	3
5. I seek out a professional "ear."	0	1	2	3
6. I plunge myself into work.	0	1	2	3
7. I straighten or clean compulsively.	0	1	2	3
8. I think about making a major life change.	0	1	2	3
9. I daydream about escaping.	0	1	2	3
10. I eat more than usual.	0	1	2	3
11. I drink alcoholic beverages.	0	1	2	3
12. I smoke (more).	0	1	2	3
13. I take unauthorized prescription medications.	0	1	2	3
14. I take unauthorized nonprescription medications.	0	1	2	3
15. I take herbal medications.	0	1	2	3
16. I eat chocolate.	0	1	2	3

17. I go on a spending spree.	0	1	2	3
18. I gamble.	0	1	2	3
19. I whine.	0	1	2	3
20. I throw things around the house.	0	1	2	3
21. I become short-tempered.	0	1	2	3
22. I curse a lot.	0	1	2	3
23. I get into fights.	0	1	2	3
24. I disappear for a while without telling anyone where I'm going.	0	1	2	3
25. I feel I should be able to cheer myself up.	0	1	2	3
26. I get panicky.	0	1	2	3
27. I think about being someone else.	0	1	2	3
28. I doubt that anyone loves me.	0	1	2	3
29. I imagine that people think badly of me.	0	1	2	3
30. I downplay my achievements.	0	1	2	3
31. I dwell on my mistakes.	0	1	2	3
32. I doubt my abilities and talents.	0	1	2	3
33. I think I'll never feel any better.	0	1	2	3
34. I think nothing is worth the effort.	0	1	2	3
35. I wonder if there's any meaning to my life.	0	1	2	3

Score: 0–10, you handle your lows gracefully; 10–19, you're on the right track, but you could relax more; 20–35, you need to make some changes; 36 and above, it might be a good idea to get some help in handling your lows.

57.

Become a Less Aggressive Driver

There are three excellent reasons for becoming a less aggressive driver. First, when you are aggressive, you put yourself and everyone around you in extreme danger. Second, driving aggressively is stressful. Third, you end up saving *no time at all* in getting where you want to go!

Are you an aggressive driver? Try this exercise to find out. Check each statement that is true for you.

____ I rarely leave enough time to arrive at my destination without rushing.

____ I try to get into the left lane of traffic as quickly as possible.

____ I try to remain in the left lane of traffic for as long as possible.

____ I rarely check my speedometer to see how fast I'm driving.

____ I only check my speedometer when I know a police car is nearby.

____ I seldom check the maximum speed limit signs while driving along the highway.

____ I am easily annoyed by people who drive slowly, unless they're in the far right lane of traffic.

____ I find myself tailgating people who drive slowly in the speeding lane—after all, there are other lanes to choose from!

____ At night, I'll often turn my brights on a driver who is slowing me down in the speeding lane.

____ Frequently, I wait until the very last minute to move right toward my exit off the highway.

____ Occasionally, I have to cut across several lanes of traffic in order to keep from missing my exit.

____ I'll follow the rules when a police car is nearby, but as soon as it's gone I'll speed up again.

_____ I believe that, despite my tendency to speed, I am really a good and safe driver.

_____ I believe that my instincts work quickly enough to prevent me from having an accident.

SCORING AND RESPONSE

If your score is less than 5: You're probably typical. Still, it would be helpful to review the rules of the road!

If your score is 5–8: You're probably overly stressed out from driving aggressively.

What are some of your thoughts when you drive aggressively?

What are some thoughts you can use to replace the ones that are keeping you anxious?

List three specific things you might want to change about your driving style.

If your score is 9 or higher: You're endangering yourself and everyone around you! Consider putting this strategy into action *now*.

Make the conscious decision to become a less aggressive driver. Think of your time in the car as time to relax. List three specific things you can do to help you relax while you're driving.

58.

Relax

When you ask people what it means to relax, most will answer in a way that suggests that relaxing is something you plan to do later—on vacation, in a hammock, when you retire, or when you get everything done. In fact, you can relax right now!

Do you know how to relax? Complete this inventory to find out. Statements are presented in sets of three. Each one has a point value. Read all three statements and decide which one best describes your situation. Then write the point value in the space beside that statement.

1.

___ I always argue when my spouse and I make opposing plans—he should have checked with me first. (1)

___ I sometimes argue when my spouse and I make opposing plans. (2)

___ I never argue when my spouse and I make opposing plans—it's not a big deal. (3)

2.

___ Only when it matters do I compete with my coworkers. (2)

___ I never compete with my coworkers—we're all on the same team. (3)

___ I always compete with my coworkers—how else will I get recognition? (1)

3.

___ On vacation, I wonder what's going on at home. (2)

___ On vacation, I worry about the safety of my home. (1)

___ On vacation, I never worry about anything but enjoying myself. (3)

4.

___ I always worry about having a bad hair day. (1)

___ I never worry about my appearance in that way. (3)

___ Only on special occasions do I worry about my hair. (2)

5.

___ When the electricity goes out, I light candles and think it's romantic. (3)

___ Sometimes I get frightened when the electricity goes out. (2)

___ I always get angry when the electricity goes out, and I call the power company. (1)

6.

___ Bad weather occasionally bothers me when it ruins my plans. (2)

___ I always get annoyed when the weather spoils my plans. (1)

___ When the weather spoils my plans, I philosophize that we can't control it. (3)

7.

___ Sometimes when my car is in the shop, I complain about the inconvenience. (2)

___ I enjoy riding with my friends while my car is in the shop. (3)

___ I view my car breaking down as a major hassle in my life. (1)

8.

___ When I can't get tickets to a concert, I just say, "Oh, well." (3)

___ I get extremely upset when I can't get tickets to a concert. (1)

___ Only sometimes does it bother me when a concert is sold out. (2)

9.

___ After a hard day, I like to rehash everything that happened with a friend. (1)

___ After a hard day, I go over everything that happened in my mind. (2)

___ After a hard day, I cook my favorite food and know that tomorrow will be better. (3)

10.

___ Sometimes I get upset when I realize that I am going to miss a connecting flight. (2)

___ I never get upset when I realize that I'll miss a connecting flight—I know there will be another. (3)

___ I always get upset when I miss a connecting flight, and I complain to the airlines. (1)

Score: 21–30, you definitely know how to relax and not make a drama out of everything; 11–20, not bad! You turn only a few things into tragedy; 1–10, you feel that every moment needs to be dramatic. It doesn't! Say to yourself, "Drama is for the movies," then get on with your life.

59.

Adopt a Child through the Mail

No, you don't actually *adopt* a child, but you do get to help one out while getting to know them. For a small amount of money each month, you can help a child and his or her parents with the necessities of life. You can also experience the joy of getting to know that child through regular correspondence.

Think of something nice you can do for someone else. Now think about the ways in which giving brings forth feelings of gratitude. What are you waiting for?

Make a list of the pros and cons of adopting a child through the mail.

PROS

1.

2.

3.

4.

5.

6.

7.

8.

9.

10.

CONS

1.

2.

3.

4.

5.

6.

7.

8.

9.

10.

1. Think about your lists. Do the benefits of adopting a child through the mail outweigh your reservations? Why or why not?

2. Do you know anyone who has ever participated in this kind of adoption? If so, list three questions below that you would want to ask him or her. If not, you may wish to ask these same questions of someone at Children, Inc., (800) 538–5381.

3. Is there another form of altruism that is equally compelling to you? If so, list it below. Then write one step to get you started as an active participant in that charity.

60.

Turn Your Melodrama into a Mellow Drama

Many people live as if life were a melodrama, blowing things out of proportion. Take the edge off your seriousness. Remind yourself that your life is not a soap opera.

Can you turn your melodrama into a mellow drama? For each situation, fill in (a) how you might react in a melodrama, and (b) how you might make it into a mellow drama.

1. You've just finished washing your car, and it starts to rain.

    a) _____

    b) _____

2. You had your heart set on getting a certain thing for your birthday, and your loved one gives you something else.

    a) _____

    b) _____

3. You are passed over for a promotion at work, and the person who gets it has been on the job less time than you and is less experienced.

    a) _____

    b) _____

4. A member of your family takes your car out for a ride and someone runs into it.

    a) _____

    b) _____

5. Your neighbor's dog gets loose and digs up some prized plants in your garden.

    a) _____

    b) _____

6. You get fired from your job.

    a) _____

    b) _____

7. You are planning a special, romantic dinner and you burn the food.
   a) _____
   b) _____

8. You are counting on help from a family member on a household project and that person gets a broken arm the day before.
   a) _____
   b) _____

9. Your wall has a crack in it and water from a rainstorm seeps in.
   a) _____
   b) _____

10. Your home workshop project looks great, but it falls apart.
   a) _____
   b) _____

11. Your date cancels at the last minute.
   a) _____
   b) _____

12. You get dumped.
   a) _____
   b) _____

13. Your wisdom teeth need to be removed.
   a) _____
   b) _____

61.

Read Articles and Books with Entirely Different Points of View from Your Own and Try to Learn Something

Have you ever noticed that practically everything you read justifies your own opinions and views on life? This rigidity is sad, because there is so much we can learn from points of view that are different from our own. It's also sad because the stubbornness it takes to keep our minds closed creates a great deal of inner stress.

Lighten up and try to learn something new! How many of the following things have you done to stretch your mind? Check off each statement that applies.

___ Read a magazine whose political philosophy is opposite to yours.

___ Subscribe to a magazine whose political philosophy is opposite to yours.

___ Read a magazine intended for the opposite sex.

___ Read a magazine that reflects a lifestyle different from yours.

___ Read a magazine intended for a different ethnic group.

___ Read a magazine whose stated aim is to proselytize.

___ Read a magazine about a topic of which you have little or no knowledge.

___ Read an editorial by a person whose views you disagree vehemently with.

___ Read an article whose purpose is to inflame people's opinions.

___ Read a book by a person you dislike.

___ Read a book about a person you dislike.

___ Read a book that claims to refute a position you hold dear.

___ Read a book about a religion other than your own.

___ Read a book that attacks your religion.

___ Read about a health practice you find dubious.

___ Read a book that claims to have evidence of supernatural things you don't believe in.

_____ Read a book that deals with lifestyle issues you find objectionable.

_____ Listen to a talk-radio program run by someone you dislike.

_____ Listen to music on the radio that you dislike or know little about.

_____ Watch a TV show about a person you dislike.

_____ Watch a TV show that promotes an opposing point of view from yours.

_____ Watch a TV show on a topic you know little or nothing about.

_____ Watch a TV evangelist from a religion other than your own.

_____ Attend a program on a topic you know little or nothing about.

_____ Attend a talk by someone whose views you disagree with.

_____ Attend a concert of music you know little about or don't care for.

_____ Attend a meeting of a group you disapprove of.

_____ Attend a religious service of a religion other than your own.

_____ Take a course with a controversial teacher.

_____ Befriend someone whose political philosophy is opposite to yours.

_____ Date someone whose political philosophy is opposite to yours.

_____ Study a foreign culture just to broaden your knowledge.

_____ Participate in a cultural exchange program.

_____ Argue an unpopular position in a debate.

_____ Study the point of view of a declared enemy of your nation or ethnic group.

_____ Talk with people who are historic enemies of your nation or ethnic group.

_____ Participate in a program with people who are historic enemies of your nation or ethnic group.

Follow-up: Look over your empty blanks. To stretch your mind, try participating in scenarios that will allow you to fill in more of them.

62.

Do One Thing at a Time

How often do we try to do more than one thing at once? When you do too many things at once, it's impossible to be present-moment oriented. Thus, you not only lose out on much of the potential enjoyment of what you are doing, but you also become far less focused and effective.

Do you try to do more than one thing at once? Check each statement that is true for you.

____ I try to get the coffee brewing while I'm in the shower.

____ Usually, I drink my first cup of coffee while getting dressed in the morning.

____ I get a head start by making calls on my cell phone while driving to work.

____ I read the morning paper while waiting at a stop light, at a toll booth, or while I sit in traffic.

____ I listen to the stock report every morning in my car.

____ I listen to music, or even talk radio, while working at my computer.

____ While I'm at home, the TV is always on—no matter what I'm doing!

____ I often catch up on phone calls to friends while doing a household chore.

____ I like to listen to music or watch TV when I exercise.

____ When I'm dining out, or even at the movies, I carry my cell phone with me.

____ I can barely take a step in any direction at work without getting a call on my phone.

____ I have three phone lines, so now I can send a fax, make a phone call, and get my E-mail—all at once!

____ I catch up on paying my bills while I watch TV at night.

____ Before I go to sleep, I read and listen to the radio at the same time.

SCORING AND RESPONSE

If your score is less than 5: You're typical. Still, you may be losing out on the enjoyment of what you're doing!

If your score is 5–8: You're probably less focused and effective than you could be.

What are some things you can do to enhance your concentration? List some things that might help you to be present in what you're doing.

Do you find that as you concentrate on just one thing, you enjoy it more? Explain.

If your score is 9 or higher: You are *not* present-moment oriented. Try blocking out periods of time when you commit to doing only one thing. Then, think about the following.

Do you become more absorbed and interested in your activity when you're less distracted?

Do you find that you get things done more quickly and efficiently when you do one thing at a time?

63.

Count to Ten

Whenever you feel yourself getting angry, give this a try: Take a long, deep inhalation, and as you do, say the number one to yourself. Then relax your entire body as you breathe out. Repeat the same process with the number two, all the way through to ten. The combination of counting and breathing is so relaxing that it's almost impossible to remain angry once you are finished.

Use the log below to keep track of the times you feel angry. Indicate whether or not you used this strategy in the second column. Observe and record the differences when you count to ten in the third column. Do you find that counting and breathing helps clear your mind—like a mini-meditation?

TIMES I FEEL ANGRY	I COUNT TO TEN		HOW I FEEL AFTERWARD
_____	Yes	No	_____
_____	Yes	No	_____
_____	Yes	No	_____
_____	Yes	No	_____
_____	Yes	No	_____
_____	Yes	No	_____
_____	Yes	No	_____
_____	Yes	No	_____
_____	Yes	No	_____
_____	Yes	No	_____
_____	Yes	No	_____
_____	Yes	No	_____
_____	Yes	No	_____
_____	Yes	No	_____
_____	Yes	No	_____
_____	Yes	No	_____
_____	Yes	No	_____
_____	Yes	No	_____

64.

Practice Being in the "Eye of the Storm"

How nice it would be if we could be calm and serene in the midst of chaos—in the eye of the storm. It's easier than you might imagine. Begin with a harmless scenario, like a family gathering. At the onset of chaos, tell yourself that you are going to remain calm. Practice breathing. Practice listening. Be an example of peace. Later, you can practice on more difficult areas of life.

   Can you learn how to be in the "eye of the storm"? Complete this inventory to find out. Read all three statements and decide which one best describes your situation. Then write the point value in the space beside that statement.

1. At the office holiday party, I
____ make sure I shake all the executives' hands. (2)
____ have a good time, no matter who I talk to. (3)
____ hang out with my closest coworkers and complain about my job. (1)

2. My best friend has been rushed to the emergency room. I
____ demand to talk to the doctor to know what is going on. (2)
____ talk reasonably to the hospital staff to find out what is going on. (3)
____ scream and cry until someone comes to talk to me. (1)

3. If I rode a commuter bus to work and it broke down, I would
____ help passengers off and ask the driver how I could help. (3)
____ complain to the person next to me that I will be late to work. (2)
____ throw a fit. (1)

4. I have agreed to chaperon my child's field trip. I
____ feel harassed as children ask me questions and the teacher asks for help. (1)
____ ask the teacher lots of questions so I don't make any mistakes. (2)
____ offer to help out wherever I am needed. (3)

5. At a family reunion, I
____ wonder if anyone realizes we are almost out of food. (2)

___ point out to everyone I see that we are almost out of food. (1)
___ calmly alert the caterer that more food is needed. (3)

6. While waiting outside a theater or stadium to get an autograph, I
___ push and shove to make sure I am not ignored. (1)
___ wait patiently until it is my turn. (3)
___ hang around even after I've received an autograph. (2)

7. During the party for a homecoming game, I
___ get in people's way as they try to set up. (1)
___ look in all the food containers to see what people brought. (2)
___ keep out of the way but offer to help. (3)

8. My child requests to have his or her first boy-girl party. I
___ calmly help my child plan the party and explain the rules. (3)
___ feel flustered as I plan the party, thinking of all the things that could go wrong. (2)
___ tell my child to plan the party, then worry about what will happen. (1)

9. The group leader for an office project has become sick. I
___ express my anxieties about not being able to complete the project. (1)
___ tell my boss that I have doubts about our success. (2)
___ encourage my coworkers that we'll be okay, and suggest how to continue. (3)

10. Out with a group of friends one night, someone gets separated from the group. I
___ worry and think something bad has happened. (2)
___ organize my friends into partners to search for our friend. (3)
___ panic and suggest we call the police. (1)

Score: 21–30, you are able to remain calm in the most stressful of situations; 11–20, you can remain calm in some situations, but others stress you out; 1–10, you get caught up in life's unexpected storms. Try to find a calm spot to take a breath. You'll soon find yourself in the eye of the storm rather than in its rip-roaring winds.

65.

Be Flexible with Changes in Your Plans

Set the goal to become more flexible! Some wonderful things will begin to happen: You'll feel more relaxed. You may even become *more* productive because you won't need to expend so much energy being upset and worried. The people around you will be more relaxed, too. They won't feel like they have to walk on eggshells if, by some chance, your plans have to change.

Are you flexible with changes in your plans? What did you or might you do in the following situations? What might you do instead to be more flexible?

1. You've just started on some work at home, when a family member announces he or she needs to be driven somewhere important "right now."
   a) _____
   b) _____

2. You have your year-end bonus money already spent in your mind, but the bonus turns out to be less than you expected.
   a) _____
   b) _____

3. You're ready to leave on vacation when a family member suddenly takes ill.
   a) _____
   b) _____

4. You have an important out-of-town meeting to attend, but you're snowed in.
   a) _____
   b) _____

5. You plan to stay up all night to finish some pressing work, but you fall asleep.
   a) _____
   b) _____

6. You're up for a promotion at work, but instead, you are laid off.

a) _____

b) _____

7. You are at a restaurant, waiting for your date, who calls and cancels.

a) _____

b) _____

8. You are counting on help from a family member on a household project, but that person gets a phone call and leaves to meet a friend.

a) _____

b) _____

9. You are planning a quiet weekend alone, but a parent calls and wants to come over.

a) _____

b) _____

10. Your home repair project, which you've already started, will come in over budget.

a) _____

b) _____

11. You have just enough time to get to the theater, but get stuck in a traffic jam.

a) _____

b) _____

12. You have plans to attend a particular graduate program, but you aren't accepted.

a) _____

b) _____

13. You had your hopes set on having your child do something specific, but he/she is unable due to a handicap.

a) _____

b) _____

66.

Think of What You Have Instead of What You Want

One prescription for happiness involves changing the emphasis of your thinking from what you want to what you have. Each time you notice yourself falling into the "I wish life were different" trap, back off and start over. Take a breath and remember all that you have to be grateful for.

Do you focus on what you want instead of what you have? The true/false exercise below will help you isolate your problem areas.

Generally, I'm content with what I have.	T	F
I sometimes get jealous of my friends' possessions.	T	F
When I'm considering a purchase, I imagine how impressed my friends will be.	T	F
If it's new, it's better.	T	F
When I was younger, I was happier.	T	F
After achieving something I've worked hard for, I find myself disappointed.	T	F
Nothing is ever as good as it first appears to be.	T	F
If I had more money, I'd be happier.	T	F
No one is ever truly satisfied with what he or she has.	T	F
I can visualize myself several years from now as a happy person.	T	F
I've gone into debt to buy an impressive car or house.	T	F
I spend more time thinking about how things look, rather than how things feel.	T	F

1. Make a list of things in your life that bring you happiness.

2. Think about the items on your list. Imagine how your life was before you had these things. Circle the items on the list that you were once content to live without. What do the circled items have in common?

3. Make a list of things you thought would bring you happiness but left you disappointed. What do these things have in common?

4. Name something that belongs to someone else that you wish you had. Think about this person. Is he or she happier than you? What do you have that this person doesn't have? Would you trade places with this person?

67.

Practice Ignoring Your Negative Thoughts

It has been estimated that the average human being has around fifty thousand thoughts per day. Some of these thoughts will be positive; others will be negative. In a practical sense, you have only two options in dealing with negative thoughts. You can dwell on your thoughts, or you can learn to ignore them.

Do you try to ignore your negative thoughts? Here's a list of some common ones that people have. Check off the ones that you have had. How much do you dwell on them? Circle 0 for **not at all**; 1 for **a little**; 2 for **a fair amount**; and 3 for **a lot**. List any other negative thoughts you dwell on and do the same. If you have mostly 3s and 4s, you need to practice ignoring your negative thoughts.

1. I look old.	0	1	2	3
2. I look fat.	0	1	2	3
3. My clothes are a mess.	0	1	2	3
4. The house is a mess.	0	1	2	3
5. I can't organize my life.	0	1	2	3
6. I'm afraid of getting fired.	0	1	2	3
7. My friends gossip about me behind my back.	0	1	2	3
8. What a waste of time this job (class) is!	0	1	2	3
9. I really looked like an idiot when I tripped and fell.	0	1	2	3
10. Something bad is going to happen to my house.	0	1	2	3
11. My significant other really doesn't love me.	0	1	2	3
12. I'm going to be late.	0	1	2	3
13. I'm being cheated.	0	1	2	3
14. What would my mother (father) say about my lifestyle?	0	1	2	3
15. This food is pretty bad.	0	1	2	3

16. I'm not going to have anything to say.	0	1	2	3
17. I never get what I want.	0	1	2	3
18. I don't have enough time.	0	1	2	3
19. I wonder if my gift is good enough.	0	1	2	3
20. My computer really annoys me.	0	1	2	3
21. This neighborhood (city, etc.) stinks.	0	1	2	3
22. I'm going to have an auto accident.	0	1	2	3
23. I'm going to get sick.	0	1	2	3
24. I was really angry when my answering machine broke.	0	1	2	3
25. What if I get lost?	0	1	2	3
26. I'm going to lose my job.	0	1	2	3
27. My boss (or someone else) is going to ask me something I don't know, and I'll look stupid.	0	1	2	3
28. I wish my boss (spouse, partner, person I'm dating) would shut up.	0	1	2	3
29. My mother (father) really messed me up by showing up unexpectedly.	0	1	2	3
30. I might as well give up because it won't work anyway.	0	1	2	3
31. I'm going to spill something, and I'll look like a klutz.	0	1	2	3
32. I'm bored and I wish I didn't have to be here (do this).	0	1	2	3
33. Did I lock the door this morning?	0	1	2	3
34. Did I turn off the stove light?	0	1	2	3
35. The weather really looks awful today.	0	1	2	3
36. I'm no good at sports.	0	1	2	3
37. My client won't show up.	0	1	2	3
38. I'll look like a fool if I don't know the answer.	0	1	2	3

68.

Be Willing to Learn from Friends and Family

Often the people closest to us know us the best. They are sometimes able to see ways in which we are acting in a self-defeating manner and can offer very simple solutions. If we are too proud or stubborn to learn, we lose out on some wonderful ways to improve our lives.

Are you willing to learn from friends and family? Pick a person whom you feel is qualified to give you advice in each specific area of your life. Then write the advice they give you. It might prevent you from having to learn something the hard way!

Who would you choose to give you advice about

BUSINESS _____

THE ADVICE IS TO _____

PERSONAL FINANCE _____

THE ADVICE IS TO _____

TALKING TO THE KIDS _____

THE ADVICE IS TO _____

MEETING NEW PEOPLE _____

THE ADVICE IS TO _____

BUDGETING TIME _____

THE ADVICE IS TO _____

BALANCING WORK AND PLAY _____

THE ADVICE IS TO _____

EATING MORE HEALTHFULLY _____

THE ADVICE IS TO _____

GETTING MORE EXERCISE _____

THE ADVICE IS TO _____

BEING MORE/LESS ASSERTIVE _____

THE ADVICE IS TO _____

BEING A BETTER LISTENER _____

THE ADVICE IS TO _____

TAKING UP YOGA _____

THE ADVICE IS TO _____

BEING MORE COMPASSIONATE _____

THE ADVICE IS TO _____

KEEPING AN OPEN MIND _____

THE ADVICE IS TO _____

LIVING IN THE MOMENT _____

THE ADVICE IS TO _____

BEING LESS CRITICAL _____

THE ADVICE IS TO _____

BEING MORE HUMBLE _____

THE ADVICE IS TO _____

BEING MORE PATIENT _____

THE ADVICE IS TO _____

HELPING OTHERS _____

THE ADVICE IS TO _____

IGNORING NEGATIVE THOUGHTS _____

THE ADVICE IS TO _____

69.

Be Happy Where You Are

Many of us postpone our happiness. We tell ourselves we'll be happy when our bills are paid, when we get out of school, get our first job, a promotion. The truth is, there's no better time to be happy than right now.

Are you happy with where you are? Take this questionnaire. Score 10 for every statement you mostly agree with, 5 for those you somewhat agree with, and 0 for those you disagree with.

I'd be happier if

1. I made more money. ___
2. I got a promotion. ___
3. I got a better office. ___
4. I worked with different people. ___
5. I had a nicer car. ___
6. I lived in a different neighborhood (town, city, etc.). ___
7. I moved into a bigger place. ___
8. I could fix up my place exactly the way I want. ___
9. I could buy nicer clothes. ___
10. I could be in a relationship with someone else. ___
11. My significant other would massage my shoulders. ___
12. My significant other were more supportive. ___
13. My marital status were different. ___
14. I had kids (I didn't have kids). ___
15. I lost weight. ___
16. I had better muscle definition. ___
17. I could take a vacation to Hawaii. ___
18. I owned a sports car. ___

19. My relatives were easier to get along with.   ____

20. The winter (summer, etc.) were over.   ____

21. It weren't raining (snowing, so hot, etc.).   ____

22. I were doing something else right now.   ____

23. I knew more interesting people.   ____

24. I knew people who could help me more.   ____

25. I were a more important person.   ____

26. I could change my career.   ____

27. I could change my neighbors.   ____

28. I could make my spouse (partner, person I'm dating) understand me more.   ____

29. We had new elected officials.   ____

30. The officials where I live would lower taxes.   ____

31. My money were invested better.   ____

32. I could finish all of my work.   ____

33. I could achieve higher status at work.   ____

34. I could be more knowledgeable about politics.   ____

35. I could be better at my job.   ____

36. I did not have to deal with authority figures.   ____

37. I did not have to spend time with my in-laws.   ____

Score: Below 100, you're quite happy in the present; 100–190, you let regrets from the past and worries about the future sometimes interfere with living; 195–250, too often you dwell in the past or worry about the future; above 255, you are in great need of finding ways to stay in the present and see your life as worthwhile.

70.

Remember That You Become What You Practice Most

Whatever you practice most is what you will become. If you are in the habit of being uptight, defensive, or acting like life is an emergency, then your life will be a reflection of this type of practice. On the other hand, you can choose to bring forth your qualities of compassion, patience, kindness, and humility—again, through what you practice.

Do you put into practice what you want your life to stand for? Read each statement below. Then check the emotion that best applies to you in that situation.

1. A colleague gets a promotion.

___ angry ___ sad ___ stressed ___ happy ___ accepting ___ understanding

2. You get a new project.

___ angry ___ sad ___ stressed ___ happy ___ accepting ___ understanding

3. Your in-laws come to visit.

___ angry ___ sad ___ stressed ___ happy ___ accepting ___ understanding

4. A friend insults you.

___ angry ___ sad ___ stressed ___ happy ___ accepting ___ understanding

5. You don't like a friend's new boyfriend/girlfriend.

___ angry ___ sad ___ stressed ___ happy ___ accepting ___ understanding

6. Your parents wonder why you never call.

___ angry ___ sad ___ stressed ___ happy ___ accepting ___ understanding

7. You and your spouse have an argument.

___ angry ___ sad ___ stressed ___ happy ___ accepting ___ understanding

8. A neighbor accuses you of being inconsiderate.

___ angry ___ sad ___ stressed ___ happy ___ accepting ___ understanding

9. A colleague takes credit for your work.

___ angry ___ sad ___ stressed ___ happy ___ accepting ___ understanding

10. You get stuck in an elevator.

___ angry ___ sad ___ stressed ___ happy ___ accepting ___ understanding

11. Something you'd been looking forward to gets canceled.

___ angry ___ sad ___ stressed ___ happy ___ accepting ___ understanding

12. Your car is still in the shop after a week.

___ angry ___ sad ___ stressed ___ happy ___ accepting ___ understanding

13. Your boss tells you that she or he wants to speak to you right away.

___ angry ___ sad ___ stressed ___ happy ___ accepting ___ understanding

14. You discover that a new friend has an annoying habit.

___ angry ___ sad ___ stressed ___ happy ___ accepting ___ understanding

15. Someone unexpectedly tells you that he or she loves you.

___ angry ___ sad ___ stressed ___ happy ___ accepting ___ understanding

Count up the check marks.

- *Angry, sad,* and *stressed* are negative emotions. If most of your checks have been placed in those spaces, you might want to practice some more positive responses to the people and events that surround you.

- *Happy, accepting,* and *understanding* are positive emotions. If most of your checks have been placed in those spaces, you're on the right road to living a less stressful life!

71.

Quiet the Mind

A quiet mind is the foundation of inner peace. And inner peace translates into outer peace. In as little as five to ten minutes a day, you can train your mind to be still and quiet. This stillness can be incorporated into your daily life, giving you greater perspective to see things as "small stuff" rather than as emergencies.

Do you know how to quiet the mind? Here are some suggestions.

1. Take a deep breath and think about a soothing place. It could be someplace you've been as a child or a place that exists only in your mind's eye. Close your eyes for a moment and visualize it.
Now write down what you see.

2. Take another deep breath. How does this special place smell?

What sounds do you hear?

Do you see yourself in this place? If so, what are you doing?

3. Write down anything else that makes this calming place so special for you.

4. Make a list of other places and thoughts that soothe your mind. Think of them whenever you need a little peace and quiet.

5. In the space below, draw a simple picture of your quiet place. Or draw a smooth, flowing shape. Project yourself into the picture and into a quiet place where you can rest your mind.

72.

Take Up Yoga

Yoga is an extremely popular and effective method for becoming a more relaxed person. It's easy to do and takes only a few minutes a day. What's more, people of virtually any age and fitness level can participate.

Have you ever tried taking up yoga? The true/false exercise below will help you isolate your misconceptions in thinking about—and resisting—taking up yoga.

I think yoga is hard to do.	**T** **F**
I think yoga takes a lot of time.	**T** **F**
I think you need to be athletic to do yoga.	**T** **F**
I think only young, agile people can do yoga.	**T** **F**
I think you need to join a gym in order to do yoga.	**T** **F**
I think you can learn yoga only from a special trainer.	**T** **F**
I think you need a lot of space and equipment to do yoga.	**T** **F**

If you answered *true* to any of these questions, think again! The answer to all of them is *false*. Anyone can do yoga, whether you are young or old, in shape or out of shape. Yoga can be performed anywhere—at home, in the office, or at a gym, if you prefer. And yoga doesn't take long, nor is it difficult. You don't need to buy fancy running shoes or expensive workout clothes. A few minutes a day of some simple exercises will provide amazing benefits.

Of course, you can learn yoga by taking special courses. Many gyms and community centers offer yoga classes. But if you want to start today and at your own pace, you can also learn yoga through instructional videotapes and books. Pop in the video, and your instructor will appear before you, ready to show you the benefits of yoga.

What benefits do you think you can gain from practicing yoga? Circle T (**true**) or F (**false**) to each of the statements below.

Yoga can strengthen muscles.	**T** **F**
Yoga can make my body more flexible.	**T** **F**

Yoga can help me reduce stress.	**T**	**F**
Yoga can instill in me a feeling of peace.	**T**	**F**
Yoga can clear my mind.	**T**	**F**
Yoga can improve my stamina.	**T**	**F**

All of these statements are, of course, *true*. For many people, yoga is an excellent way to reduce stress, to feel calm, to improve concentration and focus, and to limber up the body.

Should *you* try yoga? Circle T (**true**) or F (**false**) to each of the statements below.

I would like to feel more relaxed.	**T**	**F**
I would like to reduce stress.	**T**	**F**
I could use a few minutes of quiet time each day.	**T**	**F**
I would like to feel more at peace.	**T**	**F**
I would like my body to be stronger.	**T**	**F**

If you answered *true* to most of these questions, then perhaps you should give yoga a try!

73.

Make Service an Integral Part of Your Life

If one of your goals is to help others, you will find the most appropriate ways. Your chances to be of service are endless. You'll find that as you give more freely of yourself, you will experience more feelings of peace than you ever thought possible. Everyone wins, especially you.

Is service a part of your life? How many of the following have you done during the past year? Check off all that apply. What others do you think you could check off during the coming year?

____ Took the time to listen

____ Gave someone a hug when it was needed

____ Helped someone with homework

____ Helped up someone who fell

____ Donated money to a charity

____ Donated time and energy to a charity

____ Donated goods to a charity

____ Helped someone lift something heavy

____ Gave directions

____ Returned something to someone who dropped it

____ Helped look for something lost

____ Were emotionally supportive to someone

____ Gave up your seat

____ Put someone up in your home

____ Shared something you know

____ Taught someone how to do something

____ Helped fix something broken

____ Did a chore for an elderly person

_____ Visited someone sick

_____ Prepared food for someone sick

_____ Mentored someone at work

_____ Helped someone find work

_____ Helped someone overcome a fear

_____ Helped plan a party for someone

_____ Gave a loved one time off

_____ Watched a child so a frazzled parent could have time off

_____ Did a chore for a neighbor without mentioning it

_____ Looked after a vacationing neighbor's house

_____ Looked after a vacationing neighbor's pet

_____ Drove a nondriver somewhere

_____ Guided a blind person

_____ Recorded for the blind

_____ Lent someone something he or she needed

_____ Woke someone up who would have overslept

_____ Stayed up with someone who needed company

_____ Helped settle an argument

_____ Volunteered for community service

_____ Served on a committee in an organization

_____ Ran for an office in an organization

74.

Do a Favor and Don't Ask for, or Expect, One in Return

When you do something nice for someone, just to do it, you'll notice a feeling of ease and peace. Just as exercise releases endorphins in your brain that make you feel good physically, your acts of loving kindness release the emotional equivalent.

Have you done something nice for someone lately? Think about the following.

1. Think about the last nice thing you did for someone.

    a. What did you do? For whom?

    b. How did it make you feel to do something nice?

    c. How did the person react?

    d. What did you expect to get in return?

2. Think about the last nice thing someone did for you.

    a. What was it? Who did it?

    b. How did this act of kindness make you feel?

    c. Did you do something in return?

3. Think about five nice things you could do for the people around you over the next week or so. List them here.

    a.

    b.

    c.

    d.

    e.

4. After you complete each act of kindness, think about how you feel. Write your feelings here.

    a.

    b.

c.

d.

e.

5. Think about what you expect to get in return. Be honest with yourself. Write about your expectations here.

If, after a lot of thought, you've still left this space blank, good for you! You're on your way to eliminating one more area of stress in your life!

75.

Think of Your Problems as Potential Teachers

Problems come in many shapes, sizes, and degrees of seriousness. They present us with things that we wish were different. But when we accept our problems as an inevitable part of life, when we look at them as potential teachers, it's as if a weight has been lifted off our shoulders.

Can you think of your problems as potential teachers? Think about each potential problem below. In the space to the right of each one, write about how it can become a learning experience.

THE PROBLEM IS THIS: HERE'S WHAT IT CAN
                                                              TEACH:

Your car breaks down and
won't be ready for a week.

The cable goes out on
your TV.

You are handed a big
project at work with a
tight deadline.

Your doctor tells you that
you have high cholesterol.

You get rejected for a bank
loan to consolidate your
debts.

You are seeing someone new, who enjoys something that in the past you have always disliked.

Your neighbor wakes you up early every Saturday morning as she does her chores.

You finally decide to register for a continuing ed course you've always wanted to take—but the class is filled for the semester.

You're planning a weekend getaway when a niece or nephew suddenly informs you that he or she is coming to town that weekend and needs a place to stay.

Now write about one specific problem you've had lately. Don't forget to write about what you learned from it.

76.

Get Comfortable Not Knowing

The truth is, we *don't* know what's going to happen—we just think we do. Often we make a big deal out of something. Most of the time we are wrong. If we keep our cool and stay open to possibilities, we can be reasonably certain that, eventually, all will be well.

Are you comfortable not knowing? Complete this inventory to find out. Read all three statements and decide which one best describes your situation. Then write the point value in the space beside that statement.

1. I have a fight with my boss, and I don't know what will happen with my job.
___ I might worry about the ramifications until my boss and I talk again. (2)
___ I won't worry about the ramifications at all; it won't help. (3)
___ I will worry about the ramifications until my boss and I talk again. (1)

2. I witness a fight between my parents, and I don't know what will happen next.
___ I imagine my parents are getting a divorce. (1)
___ I get the name of a marriage counselor to give to them. (2)
___ I reason that perhaps my parents just needed to clear the air. (3)

3. My boss is leaving for a new job, and I don't know how that will affect my position.
___ I plan to make a good impression to welcome my boss's replacement. (3)
___ I think maybe it's time for me to get a new job, too. (2)
___ I convince myself that my new boss will replace me with a friend. (1)

4. My spouse is offered a job transfer, and I don't know what we should do.
___ I calmly talk over our options with my spouse. (3)
___ I become hysterical thinking about adapting to a new life. (1)
___ I play the martyr and tell my spouse to make the decision. (2)

5. The resort I really want to visit on vacation is closed for renovations, and I don't know what the other hotel is like.
___ I'm disappointed, but I go with no expectations. (2)

___ I'm disappointed, but I keep an open mind—this hotel could be even better! (3)

___ I'm disappointed, so I cancel my trip. (1)

6. My car has finally broken down for the last time, and I'm not sure about a new car.

___ I loved my old car, and I'll never get used to driving another car. (1)

___ I loved my old car, but it's time to move on. (2)

___ I loved my old car, but I can't wait to drive something new. (3)

7. My office is changing over to a new computer system, and I don't know how to use it.

___ I'm excited about learning something new. (3)

___ I grudgingly agree to take a computer course. (2)

___ I refuse to learn the new system—I'll never understand it. (1)

8. The restaurant is out of my favorite entree, and I don't know what to order.

___ If I order something else, I might not like it. (2)

___ If I order something else, I might actually enjoy it. (3)

___ I don't want anything else, so I leave the restaurant. (1)

9. My best friend makes me go to a party, and I don't know what to expect.

___ I know I'm going to have a miserable time. (1)

___ There is a 50 percent chance that I won't enjoy myself. (2)

___ I'll have a good time, no matter who is at the party. (3)

10. I receive a receipt for a certified letter, and I don't know what it could be for.

___ I'll never know if it's good news or bad news until I open the letter. (3)

___ I'm sure it's bad news, but I open the letter anyway. (2)

___ I'm sure it's bad news, so I refuse to sign for the letter. (1)

Score: 21–30, you know how to go with the flow; 11–20, you still need to work on not letting the unknown get you excited—roll with the punches; 1–20, the unknown makes you fearful and anxious. Tell yourself things will work out okay. Chances are, they will.

77.

Acknowledge the Totality of Your Being

Many of us often deny the parts of ourselves that we deem unacceptable. But when you acknowledge the less than perfect parts of yourself, something magical begins to happen. Along with the negative, you'll also begin to notice the positive, the wonderful aspects of yourself that you may not have given yourself credit for.

Do you treat yourself with loving kindness and great acceptance? Try the following to find out. Read each situation. Then circle T (**true**) or F (**false**) as it applies to you. Be honest with yourself!

I scold myself when I can't accomplish a simple task, like following a recipe.	T	F
I feel extremely stressed out when people expect too much of me.	T	F
I feel unaccountably dejected when someone points out a flaw I have.	T	F
I become extremely frustrated when I don't understand something that I feel I should know or understand.	T	F
I find that I get in a bad mood when people don't react to something as I had hoped.	T	F
I feel terrible for days after I inadvertently embarrass someone or say something I shouldn't.	T	F
I feel extremely sad when friends make plans without me, no matter the reason.	T	F

If you answered mostly *false* to these questions, good for you! You don't let small things bother you, and you seem to have your negative feelings under control.

If you answered mostly *true* to these questions, realize that these feelings are a part of who you are. Now you can try to stop them when they get out of hand!

78.

Cut Yourself Some Slack

Don't worry about being perfect! There will be many times when you lose it, when you revert to being uptight, frustrated, stressed—get used to it. When you lose it, just start again. See your mistakes as learning opportunities.

Can you cut yourself some slack? Check off people, situations, or things that have caused you to lose it over the last year. Write what you learned from each incident.

MOTHER _____

FATHER _____

SIBLING _____

GRANDPARENT _____

AUNT OR UNCLE _____

COUSIN _____

CHILD _____

GRANDCHILD _____

SPOUSE _____

EX-SPOUSE _____

SOMEONE YOU'RE DATING _____

PET _____

A RELIGIOUS LEADER _____

NEIGHBOR _____

FRIEND _____

DOCTOR _____

STORE CLERK _____

DELIVERY PERSON _____

REPAIR PERSON _____

WAITER _____

TELEPHONE SALESPERSON _____

PANHANDLER _____

BOSS _____

COMPUTER _____

CAR _____

APPLIANCE _____

BAD WEATHER _____

TRAFFIC JAM _____

TRAVEL SNAFU _____

DROPPING SOMETHING _____

MISPLACING SOMETHING _____

RESERVATIONS SNAFU _____

RUNNING OUT OF TIME ON A PROJECT _____

BEING LATE FOR SOMETHING IMPORTANT _____

NOT BEING ABLE TO FIGURE SOMETHING OUT _____

BEING BLAMED UNJUSTLY _____

FEELING SICK _____

FEELING DEPRESSED _____

79.

Stop Blaming Others

When something doesn't meet our expectations, many of us think it must be someone else's fault. *Blaming* has become extremely common in our culture. It leads us to believe we are never completely responsible for our own actions, problems, or happiness.

Think of a time when you've blamed each of the following people in your life. Tell what you blamed them for. Now consider your own accountability. Write about it below.

ASSISTANT _____

MY OWN ACCOUNTABILITY _____

CO-WORKER _____

MY OWN ACCOUNTABILITY _____

BOSS _____

MY OWN ACCOUNTABILITY _____

BEST FRIEND _____

MY OWN ACCOUNTABILITY _____

SPOUSE _____

MY OWN ACCOUNTABILITY _____

EX-SPOUSE _____

MY OWN ACCOUNTABILITY _____

CHILDREN _____

MY OWN ACCOUNTABILITY _____

MOTHER _____

MY OWN ACCOUNTABILITY _____

FATHER _____

MY OWN ACCOUNTABILITY _____

1. Does acknowledging your own accountability help you regain your sense of personal power? Does it help you to see yourself as a choice-maker? Why or why not?

2. Use the space below to create your own "accountability checklist." Think about the things in your life over which you have the ultimate control. Here are a few ideas to get you started:

   1. *I take responsibility for my personal happiness.*
   2. *I take responsibility for the way I react to others.*

80.

Become an Early Riser

Contrary to popular logic, a little *less* sleep and a little more time for you might be just what you need. An hour or two that is reserved just for you—*before* your day begins—is an incredible way to improve your life. All of a sudden, books get read, meditation gets done, the sunrise can be appreciated. The fulfillment you experience more than makes up for any sleep you miss.

Are you an early riser? If not, then think about the following.

1. Think about your morning routine. How do you spend this time?

2. Think about your favorite activities. List at least a dozen things you like to do. Circle the ones that you don't have time for.

3. Think about setting your alarm clock to ring an hour or two earlier in the morning. Describe how you feel at the prospect of having less time to sleep. (Revisit this question after you've tried this new lifestyle for a week or two!)

4. Now think about how you might use this time. Below, list the things you'd like to do *before* your day begins. Remember, there's nothing you absolutely *have* to do. Do whatever you want!

5. Next week, revise your list, adding new things you'd like to do. Revise your clock, too—to adjust the amount of time you allocate for your morning schedule. Keep revising until you've found your own comfort level.

   Remember that this simple, practical strategy can help you discover a more peaceful, even a more meaningful life.

81.

When Trying to Be Helpful, Focus on Little Things

Sometimes our plans to do great things at some later time interfere with our chances to do little things right now. By taking great care in doing something—anything—you will feel the joy of giving and will help to make the world just a little bit brighter.

Can you focus on the little ways of giving? Think about a time or place you helped someone or did something in connection with the following.

DISABILITY _____

_____

SICKNESS _____

_____

OLD AGE _____

_____

HUNGER _____

_____

LEARNING _____

_____

ENVIRONMENT _____

_____

GARBAGE OR LITTER _____

_____

REPAIRS _____

_____

TRANSPORTATION _____

_____

DOING SOMETHING AT WORK _____

_____

HELPING SOMEONE FIND WORK _____

_____

LODGING _____

_____

EMOTIONAL PROBLEM _____

_____

EVERYDAY PROBLEM _____

_____

HELPING AN ANIMAL _____

_____

SETTLING A DISAGREEMENT _____

_____

GETTING PEOPLE TOGETHER _____

_____

LOCATING A LOST OBJECT _____

_____

WORKING FOR AN ORGANIZATION _____

_____

GIVING MONEY _____

_____

82.

Remember, One Hundred Years from Now, All New People

A hundred years from now we will all be gone from this planet. This idea can fill us with needed perspective during times of perceived crisis or stress.

Make a list of all the things you can think of that you agonized over during the past year. Decide which ones will seem important a hundred years from now. Write N for **not** (important), P for **possibly**, or Y for **yes**.

83.

Lighten Up

These days, it seems that almost all of us are too serious. People are frustrated and uptight about virtually everything. Very simply, we want things to be a certain way, but they're *not* a certain way. Life just is as it is. By accepting this, you become free. To hold on is to be serious and uptight. To let go is to lighten up!

Do you take your life too seriously? You can lighten up by thinking about the following:

1. The last time you were late or waited for someone who was late, what did you do? What were the consequences?

   How might you handle the lateness next time?

2. You ate dinner out and hated the food. What did you do?

   The next time, what might you do instead?

3. A child did something in your presence that you thought was inappropriate. What did you do?

The next time, how might you act toward such a child?

4. In a presentation at work, you made a mistake that was pointed out by a coworker. How did you react?

The next time, what might you do instead?

5. Your car broke down and you missed an event that you had looked forward to. How did you behave?

What might you do the next time?

6. You got home from the store and discovered something was missing. What did you do?

How might you react the next time?

7. You forgot or lost your keys and were locked out of your house. What did you do?

   What might you do the next time?

8. The clothes you were planning to wear to a special event were not ready at the dry cleaner, or you forgot to pick them up. How did you behave?

   What could you think of doing the next time?

9. You didn't send back a response in time and missed an important deadline. What did you do?

   What might you do the next time?

10. You couldn't think of an answer for one of the questions above. What did you do?

    What might you do instead?

84.

Nurture a Plant

One requirement for inner peace is to learn to love unconditionally. The problem is, it's really hard to love a person, any person, unconditionally. A plant, however, is easy to love just the way it is. Nurturing a plant offers an opportunity to practice unconditional love.

Are you able to offer unconditional love? Think about the following.

1. When was the last time you were able to love something or someone unconditionally? What circumstances made it possible?

2. Practice extending that feeling to something or someone else. Notice what is standing in the way. How can you remove the obstacle(s)?

3. Think of a person you love. Make a list of things you don't like about that person. Then make a list of things you do like. Each day focus on one item on your "do like" list, trying to ignore any of the items on your "don't like" list.

4. Think about someone you don't like. Make a list of things you don't like about that person. Can you come up with any things you do like? Can you focus on any of the things from the "do like" list while trying to ignore the things on the "don't like" list?

5. Think about a group (ethnic, religious, etc.) that you don't like. Make a list of things you don't like about that group. Learn about the group by reading, renting videos, observing, etc. Review your list. Are you able to eliminate any of the items? Did you find out anything from your studies that can make you extend your love to this group?

6. Think about someone from your past with whom you found fault. Make a list of the reasons for your finding fault with them. How might you deal with the same faults if someone in your present life exhibited them?

85.
Transform Your Relationship to Your Problems

Obstacles and problems are a part of life. True happiness comes not when we get rid of all of our problems, but when we change our relationship to them. Our problems can be sources of awakening, opportunities to practice patience and to learn.

Can you transform your relationship to your problems? Complete this inventory to find out. Read all three statements and decide which one best describes your situation. Then write the point value in the space beside that statement.

1. If I had a problem with a coworker, I would
___ try to avoid my coworker to avoid the problem. (2)
___ confront my coworker and get rid of the problem. (1)
___ accept that there is a problem and not let it interfere with my job. (3)

2. If one of my family came down with a serious health problem, I think I would
___ probably collapse with despair and not know what to do. (1)
___ keep a firm chin and help my family through it. (3)
___ pretend there is no health problem—I hate hospitals. (2)

3. If a close friend suddenly developed a problem with alcohol, I would
___ pretend the situation did not exist. (2)
___ badger my friend about it every time we went out. (1)
___ try to talk calmly with my friend about the problem I had noticed. (3)

4. If I were in a car accident, I would
___ accept that there are some things in life we can't control. (3)
___ become hysterical about why bad things always happen to me. (1)
___ blame everyone around me for what happened. (2)

5. If I received notice that I was going to be audited by the IRS, I would
___ most likely be so nervous and upset that I would lose my appetite. (1)

___ rationalize that paying taxes is a part of life and call my accountant. (3)

___ wonder why things like this always happen to me. (2)

6. If a longtime boss, whom I really liked, left the company, I would

___ wish my old boss well in the new job. (3)

___ worry about my new boss. (2)

___ refuse to work for anyone else and quit, too. (1)

7. If I were expected to take on a monumental project, I would

___ become agitated and not know where to begin. (1)

___ wonder why I had to do it, but do it all the same. (2)

___ accept the project as a challenge and look forward to it. (3)

8. If my spouse brought home a friend whom I didn't particularly like, I

___ might not tell my spouse how I felt, but would stew about it for a while. (2)

___ might tell my spouse once how I felt, then try to accept the friend. (3)

___ might remind my spouse how I felt every time the new friend was present. (1)

9. If a relative asked me if she or he could temporarily stay with me, I would

___ accept my new houseguest, but lay down some ground rules. (3)

___ grumble a bit, take in my relative, and get annoyed at disruptions in my life. (2)

___ take in my relative, but make sure she or he knew what an imposition it was. (1)

10. If my spouse suddenly began working later hours, I would

___ assume my spouse was seeing someone else and become upset. (1)

___ have suspicions, but not voice them. (2)

___ ask my spouse about it and try to accept the answer. (3)

Score: 21–30, you look at your problems in a positive light; 11–20, you try to see your problems in a different way; 1–10, you need to work on how you handle your problems. Take a few calming breaths, then think of how to change your relationship to those pesky problems.

86.

The Next Time You Find Yourself in an Argument, Rather Than Defend Your Position, See If You Can See the Other Point of View First

You always take a side in an argument—yours! Yet if you see the other point of view first, you become closer to the person with whom you disagree and can often learn something new.

Are you able to see the other point of view first? Think about the following.

1. Think about a time at home when you argued with a family member.
   What was your position?

   What was the other position?

2. Think about a time when you argued with a friend.
   What was your position?

   What was the other position?

3. Think about a time at work when you argued with a colleague.
   What was your position?

   What was the other position?

4. Consider this: You are out with friends. They want to see one movie. You want to see another. What do you do?

   Read your answer out loud. Are you trying to see their point of view?

5. Consider this: You are at a party. Someone starts talking about a preferred political candidate, who is not your choice. What do you do?

   Read your answer aloud. Are you trying to see the other person's point of view?

6. Consider this: A spouse, friend, coworker, or family member tells you that they feel you are taking advantage of them. What do you do?

   Read your answer aloud. Are you trying to see the other person's point of view?

   Remember—there are two sides to every argument. Try to see the other side, and you'll not only learn something about the other person but something about yourself, too.

87.

Redefine a "Meaningful Accomplishment"

If you ask the average person, "What is a meaningful accomplishment?" the typical response would almost always focus on things that happen outside of themselves. These are not, however, the most important types of accomplishments if your goal is one of inner peace. The true measure of our success comes not from what we do, but from who we are and how much love we have in our hearts.

Can you recognize your own meaningful accomplishments? Read each situation, and apply it to an experience you've recently had. Circle T (**true**) or F (**false**) to show how the situation applies to you.

A friend and I recently had an argument. I was able to see my friend's point
of view.   T   F

A friend recently bought a new car. I was happy for him/her and did not feel
jealous.   T   F

I couldn't figure out how to program the remote for my new TV. Instead of
getting frustrated, however, I just took a deep breath and asked someone
for help.   T   F

A group project I worked on was a big success. I enjoyed the group's success
and did not call attention to my own contributions.   T   F

I woke up one morning in a really bad mood, but was able to change my
mood so it didn't ruin my day.   T   F

A friend came to me with a problem. Instead of sharing my problems in
return, I simply listened compassionately.   T   F

My best friend just got a tattoo. I hate tattoos, but was able to compliment my
friend and express excitement, despite my opinion.   T   F

I realized that I was becoming irritated with a close family member. I was able
to back up and push my irritation aside.   T   F

My spouse complained that I wasn't paying much attention to my home.
Instead of explaining myself, I listened openly and with understanding.   T   F

A friend made an insensitive comment that hurt my feelings. I decided not to dwell on it, but shifted my attention to my friend instead. **T** **F**

I was handed a large project, full of responsibility. Instead of having an anxiety attack, I looked at the project as an exciting challenge. **T** **F**

More people than I'd anticipated showed up at my party. Instead of scolding people for not RSVP-ing, I asked someone to run out for more drinks and chips. **T** **F**

I witnessed a neighbor struggling with a bag of groceries and offered to help. **T** **F**

I picked up some litter I saw on a corner in my neighborhood. **T** **F**

My boss yelled at me in front of colleagues. I understood that my boss was actually under a lot of pressure and cut him some slack. **T** **F**

If you answered mostly *true*, then you are doing a wonderful job not only in changing your attitudes, but in redefining meaningful accomplishments.

If you answered mostly *false*, don't sweat the small stuff! Keep this survey for future reference. Every month or so, take this survey again. Compare it to previous surveys. Hopefully, you'll begin to see how much your attitudes are changing. Congratulate yourself! These are truly life's most meaningful accomplishments.

88.

Listen to Your Feelings
(They Are Trying to Tell You Something)

Your feelings act as a barometer, letting you know what your internal weather is like. When you're not taking things too seriously, your feelings will be generally positive. Your negative feelings, on the other hand, are like warning lights on the dashboard of your car. When flashing, they let you know that it's time to ease up.

Do you listen to your negative feelings? Check off the ways you remember feeling during the last year or so. Fill in the occasion and what you did about it.

INDIFFERENT _____

COLDHEARTED _____

SELF-CENTERED _____

BORED _____

LETHARGIC _____

SAD _____

DEPRESSED _____

DESPAIRING _____

IMPATIENT _____

ANNOYED _____

ANXIOUS _____

FEARFUL _____

ENVIOUS _____

GROUCHY _____

ANGRY_____

HATEFUL _____

VENGEFUL _____

MANIC _____

REGRETFUL _____

ASHAMED _____

89.

If Someone Throws You the Ball, You Don't Have to Catch It

Often our inner struggles come from our tendency to jump on board someone else's problem. Someone throws you a concern and you assume you must catch it. Remembering that you don't have to catch the ball is a very effective way to reduce the stress in your life.

Are you someone who always catches the ball? Try to come up with an alternative reaction to each of the following scenarios.

1. You get a phone call from your mother, who lives alone in another town in the house where you grew up. She complains about how hard it is to clean and keep the house in good repair, and tells you how lonely she is because she can't go out at night by herself. You offer to take her apartment-hunting next weekend, but she refuses to go and gets angry that you should even suggest such a thing.

2. Your twelve-year-old daughter complains about being bored. It is a rainy Sunday and none of her friends are around. You suggest doing something together, and you come up with a long list of possibilities that includes baking, woodworking, art projects, and even renting a video to watch together. She stomps off to her room, shouting, "You just don't understand!"

3. You always pull more than your weight at work, and now you are so loaded down that for the last month you've been working every evening and at least one day each weekend. One morning your boss comes into your office with a project that someone else has been "too busy to get to" and can't do now because he's going on vacation. You say "no problem," but after your boss leaves, you admit to yourself that you feel put upon.

4. It's two weeks before Thanksgiving, and no one in your family has mentioned anything about getting together. For the last five years, you have made the feast, although you work full-time and go to school at night. You feel it's someone else's turn, but everybody always comes up with excuses such as "My apartment is too small" and "You know I can't boil water without burning it." Finally, your sister calls and hints broadly about Thanksgiving. You say, "I guess I'll make the dinner—again." You hang up, angry.

5. Your kid's Little League coach is a buddy of yours, and he's gotten you to agree to fill in if he can't make a game or a practice. Although you're happy to help him out and you also like baseball, it's your busy season in your business. After you've had to fill in eight times during a month, you've had it. You tell him off, and then you worry about your kid's spot on the team and your friendship as well.

6. You have been seeing your current girlfriend or boyfriend for several months, and you look forward to a couple of quiet evenings alone after several weekends full of parties and dinners with friends. On Thursday night, your date calls you and excitedly tells you that a friend from high school is going to be in town this weekend and she or he wants to include this person in your plans. You're worried that if you tell your date how you really feel, she or he will get angry.

7. Your high school class is having its reunion, and since you still live in the neighborhood, you get dragged to the organizational meeting. A "friend" nominates you to be in charge of getting the food, since you are in the catering business. You feel awkward because whether you select your company to provide the food or not, there are more opinions and hurt feelings than you want to deal with. But you can't think of how to get out of it.

8. Because you have a generous nature, when the telephone solicitor from a charity that you always contribute to calls to ask if you'll match last year's donation, you say "Of course," even though your cash flow is squeezed. You write the check, but are angry with yourself for being such a soft touch and try to figure out which of your bills you'll have to pay late.

9. A coworker confides that his marriage is on the rocks and he's so upset that it's affecting his work. You feel sorry for him, so you help by doing more work, having lunch with him, talking about his problems, and making suggestions that range from counseling to a recommendation of a divorce mediator. After a while, it seems he's taking over your life.

10. On vacation, you and your mate become friendly with another couple. You see each other twice after the trip. Then six months go by and you don't get together or even talk on the phone. You figure it was just one of those shipboard friendships, but then you get an invitation to their daughter's wedding. You don't want to go, but you feel you must send a gift anyhow. And if you're sending a gift, you might as well go. But you don't want to!

90.

One More Passing Show

When we're experiencing pleasure, we want it to last forever. It never does. When we experience pain, we want it to go away—now. It doesn't. Unhappiness is the result of struggling against the natural flow of experience.

Try the following exercise to develop your awareness that life is just one thing after another. Start out with the earliest happy memory you can remember. Write it down. Then think of something that happened around the same time that wasn't so good. Write that down, too. Then think of another good thing . . . and so on. The point is not to worry about getting the exact order, just to see the long stream of experiences you've had, the good and the bad.

91.

Fill Your Life with Love

Everyone wants a life filled with love. In order for this to happen, the effort must start within us. We must be a vision and a source of love.

How loving are you? Take this questionnaire to find out. Then the next time you find yourself frustrated at the lack of love in your own life, try to generate more positive feelings toward the people who are low on the receiving end of your love. Circle the number that reflects how much love you feel toward people in your life, where 1 is the lowest and 5 is the highest.

Mother	1	2	3	4	5
Father	1	2	3	4	5
Brother	1	2	3	4	5
Sister	1	2	3	4	5
Grandmother	1	2	3	4	5
Grandfather	1	2	3	4	5
Aunt	1	2	3	4	5
Uncle	1	2	3	4	5
Cousin	1	2	3	4	5
Child 1	1	2	3	4	5
Child 2	1	2	3	4	5
Grandchild	1	2	3	4	5
Spouse	1	2	3	4	5
Ex-spouse	1	2	3	4	5
Someone you're dating/living with	1	2	3	4	5
Pet	1	2	3	4	5
Your religious leader	1	2	3	4	5
Neighbor 1	1	2	3	4	5

Neighbor 2	1	2	3	4	5
Neighbor 3	1	2	3	4	5
Doctor	1	2	3	4	5
Boss	1	2	3	4	5
Coworker 1	1	2	3	4	5
Coworker 2	1	2	3	4	5
Coworker 3	1	2	3	4	5
Coworker 4	1	2	3	4	5
Coworker 5	1	2	3	4	5
Friend 1	1	2	3	4	5
Friend 2	1	2	3	4	5
Friend 3	1	2	3	4	5
Friend 4	1	2	3	4	5
Friend 5	1	2	3	4	5
Other _____	1	2	3	4	5
Other _____	1	2	3	4	5
Other _____	1	2	3	4	5
Other _____	1	2	3	4	5
Other _____	1	2	3	4	5
Other _____	1	2	3	4	5

92.

Realize the Power of Your Own Thoughts

In order to experience a feeling, you must first have a thought that produces that feeling. Unhappiness can't exist on its own. It's the feeling that accompanies negative thinking about your life. This simple awareness will be the first step in putting you back on the path toward happiness.

Do you realize the power of your own thoughts? If not, then think about the following.

1. Think about the last time you were severely unhappy. What unhappy thoughts were going through your mind?

Now think about this: Your life wasn't unhappy; only *your thoughts* were unhappy.

2. Think about the last time you became extremely angry. What angry thoughts were going through your mind?

Now think about this: Your life wasn't angry; only *your thoughts* were angry.

3. Think about the last time you felt stressed out. What were you stressed out about?

Now think about this: Your life wasn't one big stress mess; only *your thoughts* were stressful.

4. Below are some negative feelings. Think about a time when you felt each one, and write about it.

   a. irritation

   b. disappointment

    c. anxiety

    d. frustration

    e. jealousy

5. Now think about a way you could turn these negative feelings into positive feelings.

    a.

    b.

    c.

    d.

    e.

We wouldn't be human if we didn't have strong emotions. But when too many negative feelings crowd our minds, life becomes unhappy. Tell those negative feelings to take a hike; then make room for the positive feelings that will bring you happiness.

93.

Give Up on the Idea That "More Is Better"

As long as you think more is better, you'll never be satisfied. Learning to be satisfied doesn't mean you can't, don't, or shouldn't ever want more than you have, only that your happiness isn't contingent upon it. Develop a new appreciation for the blessings you already enjoy!

Do you think "more is better"? Complete this inventory to find out. Statements are presented in sets of three. Each one has a letter. Read all three statements and decide which one best describes your situation. Circle the letter. Then tally up the letters to see how many of each you have.

1. Whenever I start seeing someone new, I
___ wonder who else might be out there. (2)
___ am happy with that person. (3)
___ imagine that person is someone else. (1)

2. Whenever I get promoted at work, I
___ look ahead to what my next promotion will be. (2)
___ accept my new position and try to do a good job. (3)
___ think about how my promotion will look on my resume. (1)

3. I recently finished some renovations on my dream house. I
___ wonder what I can renovate next. (2)
___ appreciate and enjoy the renovations. (3)
___ think maybe I should sell the house for a better one. (1)

4. My garden receives honorable mention in the community newsletter. I
___ imagine how much better my garden will be next year. (2)
___ am flattered that my neighbors like my garden. (3)
___ wonder what I can do to finish better than honorable mention. (1)

5. I recently bought a new car. I
___ wonder how much I will get for a trade-in in a few years. (2)

____ love my new car and wouldn't trade it. (3)
____ regret my choice and wish I had bought a different car. (1)

6. I finally lose ten pounds. Now I
____ think I'd look better if I lost ten more. (2)
____ love the way I look and buy some new clothes. (3)
____ wish I looked like someone on television. (1)

7. If I had a short story accepted by a small magazine, I would
____ kick myself for not sending the story to a bigger magazine. (2)
____ be ecstatic to see my name in print. (3)
____ ask myself why I just didn't write the great American novel. (1)

8. My community softball team wins the county championship. I
____ tell my teammates that next year we'll be state champs. (2)
____ tell my teammates how proud I am. (3)
____ tell my teammates that we should go pro. (1)

9. I finally collect that hard-to-find movie memorabilia I've always wanted to own. I
____ look through catalogs to see what I can sell it for. (1)
____ set it in a place of honor to share with friends. (3)
____ think about what I should collect next. (2)

10. My spouse and I finally take a much needed vacation. I
____ wonder if the hotel down the street is better. (2)
____ enjoy where we are staying and wouldn't stay anywhere else. (3)
____ imagine that everyone else is having a better time. (1)

Score: 21–30, good for you! You are happy with what you have; 11–20, more still seems a little bit better; 1–10, you need to appreciate what you already have. Start right now with something that you already own or have accomplished. You'll find that life itself looks a whole lot better, too.

94.

Keep Asking Yourself, "What's Really Important?"

Take a few seconds to ask yourself this question every morning. When you remind yourself what's really important, you'll find that you're more present-moment oriented and in less of a hurry, and that being right loses its appeal. On the other hand, when you forget to remind yourself of what's really important, you can quickly lose sight of priorities.

Take a minute to check in right now. Look over the list below. On the first line, write about something related to the person, place, or thing that's really *not* important—and gets more attention than it should. On the second line, write about something related to the person, place, or thing that really *is* important—and deserves more attention than it gets!

Parent: *Low priority* _____

                 High priority _____

Sibling: *Low priority* _____

                 High priority _____

Spouse: *Low priority* _____

                 High priority _____

Ex-spouse: *Low priority* _____

                 High priority _____

Child(ren):   *Low priority* _____

                 High priority _____

Best friend: *Low priority* _____

                High priority _____

Boss: *Low priority* _____

                High priority _____

Colleague: *Low priority* _____

                High priority _____

Home: *Low priority* _____

                High priority _____

Work: *Low priority* _____

                High priority _____

Community: *Low priority* _____

                High priority _____

Personal
appearance: *Low priority* _____

                High priority _____

Diet: *Low priority* _____

                High priority _____

Exercise: *Low priority* _____

                High priority _____

Holidays: *Low priority* _____

                 High priority _____

Correspondence: *Low priority* _____

                 High priority _____

Recreation: *Low priority* _____

                 High priority _____

Vacation: *Low priority* _____

                 High priority _____

Charities or   *Low priority* _____
public service:
                 High priority _____

95.

Trust Your Intuitive Heart

Trusting your intuitive heart means listening to and trusting that quiet inner voice that knows what it is you need to do. Start by setting aside a little quiet time to clear your mind and listen. Ignore self-defeating thoughts that come to mind, and pay attention to the calm thoughts that surface. You'll find that when you respond to your intuitive heart, you'll often be rewarded with positive, loving experiences.

Start trusting your intuitive heart today. If you don't know where to get started, try these exercises below. They require that you clear your mind and really try to get inside yourself. Write your memories in the blank spaces. You'll be on your way.

1. Think back to the time before you started school. (If you can't remember back that far, think back as far as you can.) Try to remember a particularly happy moment. What made it so pleasurable?

2. Think back to preschool or kindergarten, when you had a choice to make between activities. How do you think you made a decision about what to do?

3. Try to remember a time when you were taking a school test and faced a particularly hard time deciding between two equally tempting answers. How did you decide?

4. Think of a time when you had a deadline to make and were so tired or stressed that you set aside your work for a while and were later able to resume your work refreshed. How did you know what to do?

5. Think of a time when you were doing a project (woodworking, sewing, or whatever) and you reached a snag that you were able to get out of without resorting to help from instructions or someone else.

6. Think of a physical activity that you do well. How do you know what to do when?

7. Try to remember a time when you were able to tell what was troubling someone without knowing how you knew. How might you have figured it out?

8. Think about a time when you were trying so hard to solve some kind of problem that your brain actually felt tired. You stopped thinking; then all of a sudden the answer came to you. How do you think it happened?

9. How do you know if you made the right or wrong career choice?

10. How do you know if someone seems right for you?

11. Now try clearing your mind. What thoughts or feelings come to you? What do they suggest you do to follow them? Try this whenever you believe you are "overthinking."

96.

Be Open to "What Is"

Much of our inner struggle stems from our desire to control life, to insist that it be different from what it actually is. But life isn't always the way we would like it to be—it is simply the way it is. The greater our surrender to the truth of the moment, the greater will be our peace of mind.

Are you open to "what is"? Complete this inventory to find out by checking off the statements that you believe are true of the way you think and feel.

____ I get up and it's raining. I hate the rain.

____ My favorite TV show has been preempted. I'm in a foul mood.

____ I have a project for work to finish at home. I wish everyone would stop bothering me.

____ I make a special dinner for my significant other, who leaves most of it untouched. Anger!

____ Before I go to a party, I have to find out who's going to be there.

____ I don't have a clear idea of what we're supposed to do in the meeting. Anxiety!

____ The rabbits ate the blooms off all the crocuses. Now the garden is ruined.

____ I have to wait an hour in the doctor's office, and I'm steaming mad.

____ After I work hard at something, I expect appreciation. If I don't get it, I sulk.

____ I can't help thinking that my house would run better if I could make all the decisions.

____ I'd like to play tennis (or another sport), but I won't because I'm not good at it.

____ If only I had gotten some breaks, I would be further along in my career.

____ I wish I could make my boyfriend (girlfriend) love me.

____ I wish I were better looking, and as soon as I can, I'm getting plastic surgery.

____ I gave them all that money, and look what they did with it.

____ I'm not interested in knowing what you think unless you agree with me.

____ You'd think my neighbors would know how they annoy me.

____ If only my kid would study harder, I could stop worrying.

____ They don't know how to run this city (country, etc.).

____ I don't want to hear bad news.

____ Nothing's going to spoil this day.

____ I'm upset that I don't have the stamina I used to.

____ How could my spouse (partner, person I'm dating) have embarrassed me with his (her) behavior?

____ Quiet!

____ I could have done great things if I hadn't been held back by my parents.

____ Why can't they ever clean up after themselves?

____ I can't believe you said that. You're kidding, aren't you?

____ That coach is a moron. If I were running that team, I'd do things differently.

____ I deserve better service. I'm not coming here anymore.

____ Don't tell me what you think I've done wrong. I don't want to hear it.

____ Here's what I think you should do. Isn't it better than what you thought of doing?

____ If only you knew how to play cards, we would have won that game.

____ You're right. I did say that before. But now I've changed my mind, okay?

____ They did that just to spite me.

____ If you don't do that, I'm going to leave you.

____ If you do that, I'm going to leave you.

____ The best is yet to come.

Score: If you checked off fewer than 10, you are generally living in "what is"; 10–18, you more often than not take the world as it comes; 19–28, you get hung up on what isn't; 29 and over, you are a "what if" rather than a "what is" person—you could be happier if you would accept more things as they come.

97.

Mind Your Own Business

How often do you find yourself saying things like "I wouldn't do that if I were her"? How often are you frustrated, bothered, annoyed, or concerned about things that you not only *cannot* control, but are also none of your business? One of the major reasons we focus on the problems of others is to avoid looking at ourselves.

Do you mind your own business? The true/false exercise below will help you isolate your problem areas.

I sometimes find myself gossiping about the silly things my business colleagues say and do.   **T**   **F**

I sometimes find myself gossiping about the neighbors.   **T**   **F**

I sometimes find myself gossiping about one friend with another.   **T**   **F**

I love the magazines and news shows that focus on the private lives of celebrities.   **T**   **F**

I sometimes find myself eavesdropping on conversations I overhear.   **T**   **F**

I sometimes respond to remarks made by other people in their phone conversations.   **T**   **F**

I try to encourage all my friends who buy retail to shop with me at wholesale clothing outlets.   **T**   **F**

I try to tell my overweight friends about my diets that have been successful for me.   **T**   **F**

I sometimes find it hard to understand what my friends see in the partners they have chosen.   **T**   **F**

I sometimes find it hard to understand why friends linger in unhealthy relationships.   **T**   **F**

1. Think about a time when you jumped in and tried to solve a problem without being asked.

   What was the problem? How did the person feel about your efforts—appreciative or resentful?

   On reflection, how do you feel about having involved yourself without being asked to do so?

   Would you do it again? Why or why not?

2. List three ways that you might try to recover from your need to be overly involved.

   a.

   b.

   c.

3. List three ways in which "minding your own business" might help to simplify your life.

   a.

   b.

   c.

4. List three places—of greater relevance to you—where you might focus your attention once you no longer involve yourself where you really don't belong.

   a.

   b.

   c.

98.

Look for the Extraordinary in the Ordinary

We see in life what we want to see. If you want to find fault with other people, your career, or the world in general, you'll certainly be able to do so. But the opposite is also true. If you look for the extraordinary in the ordinary, you can train yourself to see.

What extraordinary things might you find by looking closely at the following?

Write your answers in the blanks. Revisit these pages from time to time and add to them.

SPIDERWEB _____

KITTEN _____

PEBBLE _____

LIGHTBULB _____

EGG _____

BIRD'S NEST _____

FINGERPRINT _____

SNOWFLAKE _____

BRICK _____

CACTUS _____

FIRST SPRING BUD _____

CRICKETS CHIRPING _____

TELEVISION _____

BABY'S HEAD _____

STANDING UP _____

RUNNER _____

GOOSE TAKING OFF IN FLIGHT _____

SAND GRAINS _____

OCEAN WAVES _____

INSIDE OF A TELEPHONE _____

COMPUTER CIRCUITS _____

STRAND OF YARN _____

SOUND OF A LOVED ONE'S VOICE _____

PIANO BEING PLAYED _____

SMELL OF YOUR FAVORITE COLOGNE _____

OLYMPIC ICE-SKATING _____

HAND-WOVEN FABRIC _____

CANDLES BURNING _____

TRAIN WHISTLE AT NIGHT _____

RAIN ON THE ROOF _____

VEGETABLE OR FRUIT GROWN FROM SEED _____

GELATIN DESSERT _____

DUST MOTES _____

FRESH BAKED BREAD _____

FAVORITE SONG _____

SMELL OF COFFEE _____

LINE OF TYPE _____

WINDBLOWN CLOUDS _____

SUNFLOWER _____

DAWN _____

SUNSET _____

99.

Schedule Time for Your Inner Work

One principle of financial planning is that it's critical to pay yourself first. If you wait to put money into savings until after everybody else is paid, there will be nothing left for you! Similarly, if you wait until everything else is done before you start your program of spiritual practice, it will never happen.

Do you schedule time for your inner work? If not, try the following.

1. Think about some things you'd like to do for yourself, such as reading, praying, reflecting, meditating, yoga, and exercise. List them below.

2. Now list the efforts you would have to make to free up some time for each one. For example, you might have to hire a baby-sitter in order to take an exercise class.

3. Now schedule a little time each day, as if it were an actual appointment, for the things you've listed above. Write one into your appointment calendar for tomorrow. Then complete the rest of the week.

Once you've started scheduling time for inner work, you probably won't be able to imagine what life was like without it!

100.

Live This Day As If It Were Your Last. It Might Be!

None of us has any idea how long we have to live. Sadly, however, we act as if we're going to live forever. We postpone things that, deep down, we know we want to do. We come up with elaborate rationales to justify our actions, and end up spending most of our time and energy doing things that aren't all that important.

Do you live each day as if it were your last? How many of the following things would you like to do, but feel you don't have time for? What others can you come up with? Try doing one of them every day for the rest of your life—however long that is.

1. Start that book you've always been meaning to read.

2. Sew on the button that keeps you from wearing a garment.

3. Paint a room.

4. Make a child smile.

5. Spend the day with an aging relative.

6. Clean out a drawer.

7. Get a makeover.

8. Try a new food.

9. Start learning the words to a song.

10. Adopt a pet from the animal shelter.

11. Spend an hour making notes about what you'd like to do with the rest of your life.

12. Phone, write a letter, or send E-mail to a faraway friend.

13. Start growing a plant.

14. Turn off the TV and talk to the people who live with you.

15. Play a game.

16. Go dancing.

17. Take an hour and do nothing.

18. Learn something new on the computer.

19. Do an exercise you enjoy.

20. Really look into someone's eyes.

21. Find out how to get in touch with that famous person you'd like to meet.

22. Invite someone to dinner.

23. Visit that museum you always meant to.

24. Plan a vacation.

25. Get involved in a good cause.

26. Don't find fault with anybody for a whole day.

27. Don't go to sleep angry.

28. Learn something about your religion—or someone else's.

29. Start a journal.

30. Put some photos in an album.

31. Watch the sun set.

32. Oil a squeaky wheel.

33. Laugh.

34. Don't compete.

35. Bake.

36. Learn a new word.

37. Spend some time with nature.

38. Don't think one negative thought about yourself.

39. Give yourself the day off.

40. Say to someone, "I love you."